'Members of the Jury . . .'

'MEMBERS OF THE JURY . . .

edited by
Dulan Barber and Giles Gordon

Wildwood House London

First published 1976

Wildwood House Ltd, 29 King Street, London W.C.2.

ISBN 0 7045 0176 7

Typeset by Red Lion Setters, Holborn, London
Printed and bound in Great Britain by Biddles Ltd, Guildford

Contents

Introduction

The editors of this book were summonsed for jury service in 1972, one of us during the early summer, the other in the autumn. We served at different Crown Courts within London. The idea for the present book, accordingly, was born in the editors' personal experience of jury service.

Each of us approached our duty with a reasonably open mind, but also with preconceptions which, almost entirely, turned out to be misconceptions. One of us found the experience so depressing, irritating and even frightening that he maintained sanity throughout eleven days' attendance at court only by directing long nightly monologues at family and friends. Paradoxically, probably only thus was he able to assess the evidence presented without prejudice. One friend suggested that he should write a book about the experience, and he began to make notes.

The other of us found his jury experience, also of eleven days (which seems to be the average period), less bewildering – perhaps because he who was to become co-editor of this book had forewarned him of the tribulations involved! It seemed to the second of us that any book about jury service by any individual sometime member of a jury was bound to be intensely personal and thus almost inevitably too subjective and unrepresentative to cast any clarifying light on the jury system.

In conversation about our respective eleven days in court, it occurred to us that an edited book which sought to reflect as diverse a range as possible of individual reactions to jury service would be a more worthwhile exercise. In discussion with our helpful and indulgent publishers, it was decided that a quasi-formal reflection of a broadly 'representative' jury – i.e. twelve accounts of, basically, their own experience by twelve individuals – would provide a sensible format.

When we received our summonses to serve, one of the thoughts that went through each of our heads was that we should learn in advance of attendance at court as much as possible of what our precise duties were, of what was expected of us. The 'literature' which accompanies the jury summons is, inevitably, couched in officialese, and though it covers the basics of the job it is hardly illuminating. We searched in vain for a book about the jury that related to the individual's experience. There are, of course, books written by and directed at members of the legal profession, and there is an admirable Pelican dealing with the history of the jury; some of these books are listed in our select bibliography. The present volume is an attempt to fill what seems to us a real gap, and we hope it will be of interest, even value, to the following three categories of people in particular:

first, those summonsed to serve on a jury, who have neither more nor less knowledge or awareness of what is expected of them than any other 'average' member of the general public who pays rates, and who is interested enough to read about the experience of those who, until their own period of jury service, were in a similar position;

second, those who have at some time or other served on a jury, and who thought the experience sufficiently interesting to wish to know how others found it;

third, members of the legal profession, who may be surprised at the extent to which *they* are 'on trial' as far as the twelve men and women in the jury box are concerned.

In addition, we naturally hope that that mythical but – to authors, editors and publishers – essential being, the intelligent general reader, will find that the accounts printed in these pages will add to his understanding of one of the main processes of democracy in this country.

Our model jury was assembled mainly as a result of a letter which we addressed to the editors of a number of newspapers and periodicals (and we are grateful to the *New Statesman, Observer, Spectator* and *Times Literary Supplement* for publishing our plea for assistance). From the one hundred or so replies received, a list of topics which seemed to our correspondents to be relevant and important emerged, and from their initial letters to us a number of potential contributors were contacted and more detailed correspondence ensued. We regarded it as important to avoid too much repetition – a certain amount being essential because some aspects of jury service, not least the interminable and surely avoidable wasting of time (hanging may have been abolished but not hanging around: that is the jury's fate) seems to affect almost all jurors – without losing the personal responses and thoughts of the individual contributors.

It was, we felt, essential that the book should contain as much information as possible, and we invited some of our contributors to inject into their pieces where relevant facts about protocol, ritual, the law, administration, where it is useful if not essential for the student of our jury system to know what is or is not permissible within court. This should also make the book more intelligible to those who haven't themselves yet served on a jury.

Our letter to the press did not result in our acquiring twelve contributors. Sometimes potential authors didn't feel able to enlarge on their experience to make self-contained pieces; sometimes the limited nature of their experience precluded them from so doing. Further contributors were sought through the National Council for Civil Liberties and the Writers' Action Group, and we are grateful to both bodies for their assistance. The slight preponderance of professional writers among the contributors is largely a result of the W.A.G. response, and probably no one should be surprised that those who try to make a living by writing do write better than the non-professional writer. It is perhaps a pity, but certainly in our experience the case, that few members of the general public are willing to write for publication, while many professional authors want to say something in print about their period of jury service. Each of our jurymen and women writes under his or her own name which, we like to think, given the subject matter, makes for a more responsible book.

Of course, the 'jury' exhibited in these pages cannot be representative, but there is a strong body of feeling, fully expressed in subsequent pages, that real juries are not themselves particularly representative. More important, our twelve contributors do reflect, both in the type of cases they mention and in their grouses and bewilderment, a consensus of public opinion which is borne out by all the letters we received in response to our request for information. That there are no startling, famous or dramatic cases mentioned here may be regarded as a pity but it should be remembered that for every murder, for every case that receives even a mention in a national newspaper, there are hundreds which are known only to those involved. (It may be of interest that one of us expended much time and emotional energy in trying to persuade a member of the Great Train Robbery jury to contribute to the book. The juror finally and reluctantly declined, having found the experience so completely shattering and disillusioning that he couldn't bring himself to reflect on it again a few years after the event. Obviously, to be a juror on a major trial can affect you for the rest of your life.)

Opinions expressed in these pages on the courtesy or otherwise of judges and court personnel, on the length of sentences, on the efficacy or failure of the jury system are, of course, entirely personal and reflect accurately a range of views experienced by the editors during their own terms of service.

A word might be said here about the so-called oath of secrecy taken by jurors. Expert legal opinion we have taken is unanimously of the view that provided what is spoken in the jury room is not revealed during the case to the detriment of anyone involved, any discharged juror can say what he likes thereafter to whomsoever he wishes. However, in these pages all names of defendants, witnesses and members of the legal profession have been changed to avoid identification, and in certain cases the details have been altered to ensure that they are unrecognizable to readers.

Most emphatically, this book is by laymen, for laymen. Nevertheless, we thought its usefulness would be increased if it contained short pieces by or about those temporarily all powerful but to every member of a jury panel utterly mysterious figures, the jury bailiff and the court usher. These sergeant-majors of the courts can, it would appear at whim, either make the individual juror's life if not a pleasurable experience at least a palatable one, or the opposite. Bailiff and usher act as bridges between the legal members of a court of law and the jury, and we hope that the two accounts here of their roles and duties are helpful.

Finally, we thought it would be useful to invite one counsel to participate, to turn the tables on the jury and discuss what he or she feels about the jury, and how it tends to meet its responsibilities. We are particularly gratified that Miss Nemone Lethbridge agreed to act as spokesman for the Bar. Counsel, no matter what jurors may feel about their performance and attitude, are the only people in court – with the exception of the judge who addresses them briefly in his summing-up on points of law – who actually seem aware of the jury and who address it.

It is a certain outcome of any period of jury service that each individual comes away with one or two loudly buzzing bees in his or her bonnet. The editors of this book are no exception, although we have been reassured to discover that many of our own concerns have similarly preoccupied and exercised others. A few points about which we feel particularly strongly are discussed briefly at the end of the book.

At the time of writing, a select committee appointed by the Lord Chancellor is investigating the jury system. On that committee the layman, the juror himself, is not represented. If nothing else, this book surely indicates how extremely seriously and conscientiously twelve men and women who happen to have served on juries in the last few years have regarded their responsibilities. Sir Robert Mark, Commissioner of the Metropolitan Police, has complained about 'the atmosphere of sacred mystery which obscures any discussion of the jury'. Let us hope that this book will help to dispel at least some of that mystery.

London — Dulan Barber
1974 — Giles Gordon

Anthony Barker

One day some time ago, three young men were charged before Chelmsford Crown Court with having conspired to extract money with menaces from an older man. This man admitted that he liked to hang around certain places meeting boys and young men: it was a case of alleged homosexual blackmail and Mr X would appear in court. One of the three young men, the eldest, pleaded guilty and needed only to be sentenced. The other two pleaded not guilty and were sent for trial. The jury had to decide whether these two had knowingly been part of the plan to make the threat. I was on the jury – my first experience of jury service, as it was for ten of the other jurors.

We had, in this case, no stolen goods, photographs of damage or footprints or finger smudges sitting on a table in court. What these two young men had overtly done was virtually agreed. What the other one, who had pleaded guilty, had done by way of a blackmail attempt was also agreed. What was most closely argued and examined in court and in the jury room was what these two had known and been thinking while they had their contacts with the victim and what their own real purpose had been. Were they in on it? Had they guilty minds? Did they know what they were doing?

We searched for over five hours for a guilty mind in each of their cases and, by a majority of ten to two, we decided we had found one. I was one of the two jurors who thought that we had not – or, at least, that we'd not heard enough to be properly sure 'beyond a reasonable doubt'.

I had always wanted to be on a jury, partly because of being a teacher of social science. How ordinary British people make a group decision while accommodating each other's manners and prejudices must surely be the very stuff of the social and political culture. When this difficult homosexual blackmail case came up it proved to be rather more than merely interesting. It shook me.

Having received my jury 'summons' (an unfortunate way of calling citizens to their duty) and noted the quite reasonable subsistence allowances, I turned up on the appointed Monday morning at a big waiting hall – Essex County Council's official ballroom, no less. Perhaps a hundred people gathered and had their cards checked off before listening to a minute of talk from the official about the daily timetable of when to turn up in the mornings and after lunch and how to claim the expenses. After that, people started talking to each other or sat with newspapers and one or two books, as they preferred.

The nervous-looking clerk dealt with people's questions about how many hours a day they'd have to wait around before being put on a jury and courteously encouraged the business men who were trying to talk their way out of the entire procedure to submit to their civic fate.

A very fat working man of about fifty (whom I shall call Benson) walked in. He was dressed in rather worn, blue overall trousers and bib and brace with an old jacket and had his cloth cap still on his head. I immediately took him to be the boilerman come to check the radiators. Instead, he walked over to the official and queued up to present his card. People stared a little. He moved away to a far corner of the hall, well away from everyone else, approximated his vast bottom to one of the narrow canvas stacking chairs and slowly lowered himself. He rolled himself a cigarette from his tin and opened the *Sun*. He took no notice of anyone and was too far away to hear the comments or even titters from some of those who were already chatting to each other. Had this funny chap come for jury service? What a way to dress. He must be hoping to go straight back to work before the end of the day. He really was Andy Capp's uncle.

He sat like this for three days and was then called. I'd been called before then and didn't see him again, but heard later in the week, over lunch with a couple of my fellow jurors, what had happened to him.

He'd waddled off with his group to the other court room. The judge, as usual no doubt, eyed the jury as they filed into the court room, as did the barristers. He made whatever noise judges make to attract their officials' attention and was shown the jury list. 'Mr Benson,' said the judge when the jury were all seated in their box, his voice dripping with cream. 'I'm afraid you're going to be rather uncomfortable in that little box for what may be several days. If you'd like to be excused, I'm sure that would be quite understandable. Would you like to be excused?' Mr Benson paused for thought. He, like me in my jury box, had been first into the box because his name began with B. He'd eased his stomach along the front ledge of the box and finally sunk into the far corner seat. He'd waited three days. 'Thank you,' he said, 'but I've got this far and I want to stay put now I'm here.' The judge also paused, but more briefly. 'Mr Benson,' he said in a different tone of voice. 'I'm quite sure you will be very uncomfortable indeed sitting there for perhaps four or five days. Thank you very much. You are excused.' The message was received clearly and Benson began to shuffle prior to rising and edging his way out of the box. Five other jurors sharing the front box with him also got out so that the wrongly-sized (or wrongly-dressed?) juror could roll slowly out of the box and the court room, all eyes on him. Whether he'd taken off his cloth cap in court, I didn't hear. How far obesity is an objective factor in the incidence of working-class membership of juries has yet to be researched definitively.

The jury group which I was in was called into court more than a day before we were sworn in and began our own case. For some reason, perhaps to be 'broken in', we sat in the jury box, but as mere spectators, while several defendants who had pleaded guilty came up for sentencing. Once we had worked out that we were merely lookers-on (nothing had been said to us as guidance) I suppose we settled in and got used to the court room. We scrutinized our judge and all the other characters in the dramatic scene. I had heard of our judge before, but I couldn't remember why. Was he a controversial judge with public views on hanging or teddy boys or whatever? Had he sat on a Famous Case such as Justice Salmon punishing the Notting Hill race rioters? Nothing was dredged up from my memory.

Why was no trial going on, with witnesses and counsels' speeches? Of course – these people were pleading guilty so the only speeches were requests to the judge for leniency: the 'plea in mitigation' is it called?

A pleasant-looking chap about thirty had had an evening meal at the local Chinese, including about two bottles of wine. He'd managed to drive himself to the factory where he worked and to climb in by a skylight. After this exertion the red mist had descended over his eyes and when he woke up on the factory floor and was discovered, he was surrounded by thousands of pounds worth of damage to highly expensive, imported and possibly now unobtainable machinery. The violence had been formidable – materials scattered and thrown everywhere as well as the machinery in ruins, apparently by a hammer lying by him. He agreed he must have done it. He didn't remember or know why and had no grievance against his employer, for whom he'd worked only a very short time. He was really very sorry and knew that drinking wine was his problem.

All this was relayed to the judge by a particular barrister who delivered several extenuating pleas while we were in court. He seemed to specialize in them and bowed and scraped quite professionally and sincerely in the course of his brief advocacies. This must be a sub-branch of the barrister's trade which I'd not seen before. The criminal bar, tax lawyers and planning silks were all groups I'd heard of but the cringing bar was new to me. This chap was ideal. His rather craggy, Victorian face with small mutton-chop whiskers combined with the wringing of his hands, his small stature and his permanent bow towards the bench to produce an almost Dickensian picture. The sticky deference and archaic language, designed no doubt to make the judge feel older, more senior and more mellow than he really was, completed the cameo.

By great good fortune, this sweetly innocent machine smasher had a girl who wanted to marry him despite his almost certainly pending prison sentence. He wanted to marry her and was willing to bring up her small child as his own. The barrister excelled himself with this candied confection of repentance of sin, neo-marital loyalty and forgiveness, to be followed by the prospect of a new and loving family, created out of crime and disgrace. The wish would be father to the child. 'My lord, I do most humbly request my lord to give this man a chance to face up to the responsibility of marriage – marriage to this woman, this Good Woman, my lord – and to providing for her and The

Child and that the time he must inevitably spend incarcerated as his debt to society for this most serious behaviour while grossly intoxicated may be as brief as the court's duty to protect society and the value of private property could possibly allow. A better future awaits him, my lord, after this dark chapter and if it was at all possible to find within your mercy a prison sentence [at this point the extenuation barrister's art is to aim his actual request a bit below what he thinks the judge in question would probably feel disposed to give anyway] of no more than, perhaps, a limit of, twelve months, at most [his eye at this moment is not cast down in deference but is on the judge to spot any visible apparent reactions to his bid] then I am certain, my lord, that this shamed and contrite man will repay the court, and your lordship, with a blameless and worthwhile family life thereafter.'

The defendant was asked if he wished to speak and repeated what counsel had said about settling down with wife and step-child, but without table wine, and was given a very light sentence, as requested. This judge appeared not to be too bothered by massive property damage, at least by men who were blind drunk, who had no apparent evil intent and who had been thinking of marrying. So far, so good, but what did rouse him? We soon learned.

The case was remarkable and horrifying. A boy of sixteen with a decidedly vacant stare and the general look of a mentally retarded or disturbed youth pleaded guilty to several very serious indecencies and rapes. He'd climbed into an affluent suburban home one morning after the husband had gone to work and forced gross indecencies on the wife. He'd forced another married woman to drive him into the country and had raped her. There was a third case, if I remember the chilling details at all correctly. He sat in the dock between two guards, very slight and slender with no apparent interest, looking at the floor. A different barrister from the rather Dickensian one attempted an extenuating plea. He said nothing about psychotic background or mental ill-health but simply referred the judge to the reports on these matters. He stressed the truly terrible experience of the women, who had told the police they'd feared for their lives. He hoped, however, for some consideration of the defendant's sixteen years and the hope that, with normal maturity, these terrible drives would abate. He hoped for a sentence of, perhaps, some four years, if at all possible?

Without asking the youth if he wished to say anything thc judged passed sentence. The savagery and terror; your animal behaviour (pausing deliberately to turn and consult one of the women's statements), 'You placed her nipple in your mouth and sucked it.' Seven years.

There was a very short silence in the court, a small gasp from some quarter I could not see and a sudden general shuffling as the tension broke. A ripple of small movements ran through the jury box. I was watching the youth as the judge reached his actual sentence. His face registered nothing. He turned very quickly on his heel and stepped down the steep stone stairs from the dock to the cells below. There was a clatter as he took the top few stairs very quickly, then a crunch and a thud as he seemed to fall down the rest. Neither guard had restrained or supported him after he heard the sentence. He had spun round and dropped from sight. We heard later in the week a rumour that he had fainted and fallen down the steps, with no one at the bottom in case people reacted in this way to their sentences.

What was the effect of being in court for these two cases, plus one or two minor ones, on the jury? Generally, it certainly gave us time to work out what went on, which probably meant that when a barrister began to address us on our own case we took in more of his opening remarks. But, as barristers seem to follow the methods of traditional schoolroom pedagogy in imparting information and argument (you tell them what you're going to tell them, you tell them and then you tell them what you've told them), this may not have made much difference. More particularly, some of us felt we had some very limited insight into this judge's likely view of our blackmail case, when this had begun. In the opinion of two other jurors to whom I spoke later, as well as myself, he had been remarkably light on the destruction of property and very heavy on the rape case. We'd reckoned that the boy was not normal and doubted his full responsibility for his actions. I'd suggested in conversation that the seven-year sentence would be reduced on appeal, which, some time later, it was, to four years. The bringing in by the judge of salacious detail during sentencing had distinctly shocked these two others. What, we wondered, would he make of homosexual blackmail? Edgar Lustgarten had always taught us that it was the most fiendish of crimes – the making of the past weaknesses and transgressions of others into the plaything of cruel and greedy minds. Perhaps this judge would come down like a ton of bricks on young blackmailers who appeared to be of normal intelligence and understanding and who were simply out for easy money. But what would he think of Mr X? Would the judge see him as an innocent victim or as an immoral and irresponsible fool who brought this trouble on himself by his disgusting loitering around lavatories?

Having just witnessed the seven-year sentence, I decided that, for my part, I would require to see a full measure of proof beyond reasonable doubt before supporting a Guilty verdict on a blackmail charge in this judge's court. This particular judge might consider youthful blackmail to be a reprehensible but not very surprising consequence of homosexual behaviour by older and richer men. But he might consider older homosexuals to be a reprehensible but unsurprising target for the really evil crime of cold, calculating blackmail. He seemed, from the two serious cases we'd seen, to feel more strongly about serious illegality concerning sex than that concerning property and blackmail is, basically, a very serious crime. I was, therefore, primed by this court-room experience to take no chances on the exact form his possibly strong feelings might take in a case which brought homosexuality and blackmail together. I would be looking for the onus of proof where I knew the judge would tell us to seek it – on the prosecution. I hoped that the two other jurors I'd spoken with about the seven-year sentence might think likewise.

We were sworn in (I affirmed). The case began.

Tom, Dick and Harry were three young men of about twenty-four, twenty-two and seventeen. Tom, a married man, had pleaded guilty to trying to extract money with menaces or blackmail threats from the case's 'victim', to whom I shall give the fictitious name Timkins. Dick and Harry denied being part of Tom's plan; this is what the court case was all about and what we on the jury had to decide. Was there evidence beyond reasonable doubt that Dick and Harry knew of the threat when they spent time with Tom, particularly on the day the money was due to be handed over? As the judge said in his summing-up: 'Were they in on it? Did they know what they were doing?'

Mr Timkins was a business man with a wife and teenage children. It was agreed that he had homosexual tendencies and liked to meet boys or young men, and hung about public lavatories for that purpose. It was not Tom, the 'guilty' eldest defendant, whom he had met first, but the 'middle one', Dick. It was agreed that he had engaged Dick in conversation in a public lavatory and had followed him over the road, asking him if he had any young friends whom Timkins could meet. Dick told the older Tom and the younger Harry of this encounter and it was not long before Tom rang up Timkins at his office and told him that a £50 gift or 'loan' was needed or Timkins's wife and children would hear about his habits. Timkins went to the police who arranged for him to promise to hand over the money, in marked notes, personally in the street with the police watching.

Tom and Dick had paid Timkins a visit in his office, either to 'case' him for the blackmail (as the prosecution said) or to fulfil his own request for a sociable chat with Dick and to introduce Tom (as the defence said). It seemed apparent that Tom had thought of the blackmail and certain that he had made the call. Apart from this visit to Timkins, the principal occasion which produced evidence and allegations about Dick's and Harry's complicity was the afternoon spent mostly in a betting shop just across the street from the spot arranged for Timkins to hand over the money and immediately prior to this rendezvous. They had very little money between them and spent the afternoon half listening to the racing results and half talking about spending what they had on either bets or bacon sandwiches – and about Timkins and money. There were various points about who had said what, and in what conversational contexts, embedded in the three defendants' 'verbals' to the police, supplemented by the witness-box recollections of one or two habitués of the betting shop who were on hand at this time. The two counsel were to go on at great length about the meaning or implication of various phrases reported in one or other of these statements or testimonies.

At about five o'clock the rendezvous with Timkins was due and either or both Tom and Dick told Harry to go over and collect what Timkins would give him. When they met, Harry said, 'I've come to collect a packet,' and Timkins asked him to write out a receipt. Harry wrote a crude receipt for 'a packet' with a stub of pencil and took the packet without looking inside. A few minutes later all three were arrested by the watching police. They each had a 'verbal' written out for them to sign. One twist in the otherwise simple evidence was that Tom rejected his statement. He said in court that his straight incrimination of Dick in his statement had been signed under police threats. He claimed in court that he had acted alone, Dick and Harry believing that the money from Timkins was a friendly loan until one or other could get a steady job and pay him back. This twist in Tom's evidence was to have interesting consequences for Dick when the jury came to argue over his guilt.

Two impressive and convincing barristers had done excellent jobs and the judge's summing-up and legal guidance were equally good and clear. If I felt confused it was by the difficulty of deciding the truth and not by any weakness in the presentation or conduct of the evidence and trial.

We filed into the jury room and leaned against the wall or propped up the radiators. Reserve hung heavily in the plain, serviceable room. One or two of the men extended themselves to the extent of lighting a cigarette and offering one to their immediate neighbours as a means of getting started with them. Some business with ashtrays and the usual excessive English thanking of people who passed them across to the smokers. Most of the nine men and three women looked down, said nothing and perhaps came to terms with this being not a railway waiting room but a place where some relationship would need to develop between us if we were to do the job in hand. No one seemed to be weighing up the group with a view to being chosen as foreman. I'd decided I didn't want to be chosen because he might be expected by the others to be only an impartial chairman and counter of heads, whereas I wanted to be in on any arguments. So I also kept quiet and eyes down.

'Well, the judge didn't tell us how to pick a foreman,' said a cheerful-looking man. 'What do we do – draw straws?' 'Well,' said another, more rural voice, 'Who's done this sort of thing before? Been on a jury? I've never.' They both looked round the room. 'Well, yes, I have been on one before,' said a sharper voice. 'Actually.' 'Oh, well then,' said the first man, 'You know the ropes: you'd better do it.' This proposal was ratified by a short silence and people starting to take their seats around the table. How much, I wondered, was our king-maker guided by the fact that our foreman seemed to be the only one of us who had been on a jury before and how much by his instant judgment that he was the sort of chap who had better do that sort of job anyway? Our foreman was the most obviously middle-class or professional of the men present. His was the only three-piece suit: a discreet check with cutaway white collar and striped tie. Most of the other men wore sports jackets. He was what ladies once called well-groomed: short back and sides in every apparent respect. He turned out later to be, indeed, an insurance broker who commutes first-class to London from a distant and decidedly posh seaside resort. We began.

My head stayed down as the foreman took an immediate straw poll on the two defendants to see if we needed to discuss. In this first of many such ballots I got a very vague impression that perhaps as many as nine of us leaned away from conviction. I gave my 'not guilty' opinion on both Dick and Harry in a very tentative and brief manner as I had no wish to start an argument if there was indeed already a general agreement to acquit. It was impossible to be at all sure what the jury felt because so many said they wanted to hear it discussed before venturing any personal opinion. I found this very interesting. They had heard the evidence and the judge's valuable summing-up but apparently felt that they could not give even a provisional view – or preferred not to do so – until they'd heard what the others thought. If this was a genuine hesitation on the substance of the matters before us, and not a matter of people affecting a 'shy' style to preserve their privacy at this early stage of our meeting, then whoever spoke up with the right tone or emphasis might pick up these jurors' support. They would compare their own hesitant thoughts with this spokesman's bolder conclusions and join him or her because they fitted. Although they could probably not be enlisted in a direction flatly contrary to their own initial thoughts, the strength of these feelings – a greater or a lesser confidence that they had the right answer – could probably be influenced by a firm lead. They seemed to tend against conviction: would it be up to me to encourage this? Or was this impression of them quite wrong?

The foreman, at least, seemed to share it. He took a strong 'guilty' position on both defendants and became the spokesman for that side. His view was that Dick was smart and very capable. For someone like him to claim that he thought the £50 due from Timkins was a gift, or a not very serious loan, was absurd. Harry was probably also involved, but as a junior partner. The three of them had intended to milk Timkins for as long as he paid up. Tom, who had pleaded guilty, had changed his story after signing his 'verbal' statement not because he had lied in it under police threats, but because he had since agreed with Dick (either voluntarily or under Dick's threats) to try to take the rap alone. He therefore lied in the box to try to clear Dick and Harry. All three were guilty as charged and Dick was probably the boss of the affair.

We were again asked our views in turn after the speech. Having placed myself opposite the foreman I came in half way round the circuit. I said that we were not asked to strike a balance of probability in this inevitably rather uncertain business of judging the state of people's minds. We had been told to require a proof beyond a reasonable doubt, and the evidence was not there. I didn't find the three to be very savoury characters and Dick himself was clearly a very fly boy if he wanted to be. But we must seek evidence that Dick knew that the money was coming from Timkins as a result of a threat by Tom and that Harry knew anything about the money at all. I was pretty sure of Harry's innocence and not at all sure of Dick's guilt. None of us could be sufficiently sure about Dick without more guesswork than we were supposed to allow.

At this early stage the 'not guilty' group were definitely the majority. The leverage on our proceedings available to a foreman as chairman became clear. If this majority group had included the jury's foreman he could have put the onus on the 'guilty' group (only one or two jurors were really firmly of this view) to say why they should prolong discussion. When they had had their full say once more a foreman could have pointed out that it takes at least ten to produce a Guilty verdict and it therefore seemed that we should return a Not Guilty verdict without delay.

In fact, our foreman found himself in the minority and used his chairman's role to soldier on in the hope that things would change. The onus was on the majority to propose stopping the discussion and returning Not Guilty verdicts. This proposal would have been tricky because of 'fair play' to the minority – even if they would only repeat themselves in further talk – and because some of the majority group were not very sure of their views and might oppose ending the discussions. More basically, an early 'closure' proposal might have made people feel that they had not done their duty fully (or, perhaps, had their psychological money's-worth from being on the jury). The entire business had now taken up nearly five days and a discussion of a mere hour would not be a satisfying conclusion to the experience. I therefore suppressed any wish to force a closure on the foreman and no one else in the majority group raised the point. If the balance moved away from acquittal, I reasoned, there would be enough of us opposed to conviction to prevent a verdict of Guilty.

The balance did move. The foreman took us through the case and the main points put to us by the two counsel. We entered the relatively tangled business of Tom's 'verbal' which he had repudiated in court. For about three further hours, making four so far, we dwelt on the reported phrases used by Tom and Dick which the counsel had examined and cross-examined at such length, because it was about all there was to go on. We discussed the evidence from the witness box of the three defendants, of Timkins, of the police officer and of the other men in the betting shop.

It was genuinely difficult. If Tom or Dick appeared to have agreed that they could 'con' Timkins, did they mean a blackmail plan or only that he was likely to prove a useful contact for getting a job and perhaps also a sucker who would fairly willingly do them favours (including gifts of money) now and then, in the hope of sexual favours or introductions to other young men? If Dick did have some general idea of using his knowledge of Timkins's weakness to extract favours in the indefinite future, did this constitute an intention to blackmail him now? Where was the evidence, even from Timkins himself, that Tom's plan was known, let alone actively supported, by Dick? The Nixon tapes have since made us more familiar with the problems of interpreting 'Yes,' or 'Right, fine,' when one person in a reported conversation is reacting to points made by another.

I am not, of course, an objective reporter of our discussion but I felt that these reservations from the 'not guilty' group were increasingly met with general assertions of the untrustworthiness of Dick, rather than particular answers to points. Several jurors changed sides on Dick's guilt and one juror justified his switch in his own eyes by becoming the most certain of the 'guilty' group. While trying not to repeat myself too much, I plugged away at the guidance the judge had given us on conspiracy and blackmail. I realized that the 'burden of proof' argument would seem a bit theoretical and tried to keep off it, although this was difficult when the foreman (as I felt) kept on offering suspicion and distrust of Dick rather than citing incriminating points from the trial. I had a couple of disagreements with the foreman on what the judge had said on the legal points and did not amuse him (and may not have won ground with other jurors) by reading out verbatim sentences from the summing-up from my notes. The foreman could say only that he recollected differently so I suggested that we return to court for further guidance on the law of conspiracy and (I managed to add) on the burden of proof and the 'guilty mind' problem.

This was agreed and we told the usher outside the room that we wanted to write to the judge. Paper and envelope were produced and we settled the text of our questions, written out by the foreman. After a few minutes we were told that the court would reassemble. When we trooped back into our jury box, everyone else except the judge was waiting for us. He entered in the usual way, with the court 'upstanding', and conveyed to the court what questions we had asked before making comments. He said we should ask again if we were still not quite clear on these points. He withdrew and we filed back to our room.

I was pleased with our excursion because the judge had now clearly repeated all these points I had been quoting from his summing-up speech. We did not have to be completely convinced, but satisfied beyond a reasonable doubt that either or both Dick and Harry knew of the blackmail threat and were supporting it by their conduct. It was for the prosecution to establish this and not for the defence to dispel the doubt.

On returning to our room, I felt that there was little more anyone could say and the initiative lay with the foreman as chairman. Perhaps it was the judge's further advice which encouraged him to throw Harry to the lambs. He now reckoned him innocent notably because, as I'd maintained, a guilty blackmailer does not stand in the open street while picking up the money, writing receipts for 'a packet' in a slow hand. The foreman decided that Harry was not very bright and had probably been only a runner. This was generally agreed. But he could not see Dick as a mere friend of Tom's who happened to be in the betting shop when Tom was waiting for Timkins to come along with the money. I'm not sure how far I think the foreman's decision to let Harry go was a kind of compromise or gesture of reasonableness in order to nail Dick. It certainly had that effect, or so I thought, on some of the 'guilty' group who were, by now, about eight strong. The idea that one has, rather mercifully, let one defendant off, but must now be doubly sure of getting the other, seemed to appeal to one or two jurors, although such an idea had more to do with their egos than with the evidence. I think the foreman was less guided by this psychological point than by his view of the evidence which I, of course, regarded as being a bit general and touched with personal feelings about Dick's possible character. Having dropped Harry, he did, however, emphasize his view that Dick was not only a conspirator but the leader of the affair. The foreman reckoned that Dick had got Tom to make the phone call and had now somehow got him to take the rap. I said that this was pure speculation.

It was now largely a matter of me versus the foreman. Clearly, we should bring it to an end soon. After yet another straw poll the 'not guilty' group on Dick was down to three and one of us promptly moved over in order to produce a decision. We were all tired and there was nothing one could have said to this chap about the case as his switch was solely to end the discussion: he said he acted out of respect for the majority. The foreman asked me and the other remaining juror (a lady who had said nothing in five hours except that she thought them both not guilty and agreed with my points) whether there was a chance of us changing to make it a unanimous decision. We said no, so he began a note to the judge asking him (or telling him, as it was past the appointed minimum time allowed for a majority verdict) that we were split ten:two on at least one of the counts. We took formal votes and found Dick guilty by ten:two on conspiracy; we found Harry guilty of technically receiving the packet and not guilty on the major charge.

I had been the main protagonist for the 'not guilty' (that is, 'not proven') view and had apparently started with some eight allies. I ended with one, albeit a very firm one, having lost the last who had switched simply in order to end the business. I'd tried very hard not to talk too much and to keep to a conversational style with only one point per short sentence. I was a bit confused by some of the evidence, did not feel I knew the truth but was not going to help convict Dick on the basis of his being a not very attractive personality who would clearly make an effective liar if he so chose. I was also mindful of the seven-year sentence we had seen handed down to the rape boy and was determined to require a proper degree of proof before joining in a verdict which might produce an unjustifiably harsh punishment. Our debate had been a good one with no lazy nonsense based on crude personal or class prejudice, views about middle-aged queers or outrage that someone should accuse the police of fixing a 'verbal'. If people had such thoughts, they stayed under cover. The foreman had pushed for his view, and won, but had been a good chairman, notably in his taking us through the case to establish points of agreement. If I felt he'd judged Dick's possible character rather than the evidence against him, he would himself claim that he had simply interpreted the evidence a little differently from me and had been more willing to 'read in' some of the inevitable gaps with his judgment of what was likely. I would have been willing to do that to complete a personal judgment that someone was guilty beyond reasonable doubt, but not to make such a judgment. Perhaps in return for dropping Harry, the foreman had moved from having a couple of allies to nine on Dick's case.

After our verdicts were delivered, the judge sentenced Harry for the minor offence of receiving (I think he got probation or a conditional discharge) and gave Dick only about sixteen months. Perhaps the majority verdict of ten:two and any personal feelings of the judge based on the fact that Timkins had made the initial approaches to the two young men were factors in a possibly rather light sentence for this crime. In delivering sentence, the judge did not go in very much for the 'most odious crime' routine to which the prosecuting counsel had treated us in his earnest speach. (Several jurors also noticed that, throughout the trial, the defence counsel took no notice whatever of the prosecution's request, sanctioned by the judge, that Timkins be called Mr X in open court; interestingly, neither the judge nor the prosecuting counsel himself pulled him up about this.) Tom got a bit more than Dick, but still on the light side for blackmail, I thought: there was no majority verdict on him so perhaps the judge was, indeed, of the opinion that if older men begin these relationships, younger men are bound to be tempted to exploit them.

I had urged, but not much expected, my fellow jurors to require proof beyond a reasonable doubt because that is the rule. The judge had said so several times and I'd quoted him several times. I'd hoped to sway them with his authority but they seemed to see the making of a decision as their paramount job. If it had to be made on a balance of probability, so be it. The official English tradition of returning a doubtful 'not proven' case as a Not Guilty verdict did not seem to interest them. It was their job to decide – to plump – if necessary even, perhaps, to guess. A judgment of characters – defendants, witnesses, police, even counsel – was the main available basis for doing this if the actual evidence was scarce because of the type of crime in question.

No doubt only a naive person should be surprised by this. It is probably the first finding of the research on juries now building up in America and elsewhere. If it is, or if judges and barristers know quite well from their experience that juries don't apply this judicial and constitutional precept, why do they go on intoning it? It's not an easy idea for many people to grasp. The vast majority of jurors, I would guess, believe that they are being asked to decide whether 'he did or didn't do it'. This is a balanced, symmetrical model in the mind's eye, very similar to the 'two sides' of any judgment, to choosing between two lots of politicians in an election or to a lawsuit in which judgment must be for either plaintiff or defendant. Certainly in England and Wales, where the Scottish verdict of 'not proven' is unknown, all these matters of public business and affairs are based on a 'zero sum' idea that if one side wins, the other side must, by the same token, lose. To say that you think a person is probably, on balance, guilty as charged but there is not proof 'beyond a reasonable doubt' is to try to embrace an unfamiliar and even odd asymmetry. It's like saying that Labour is best for the country but voting Conservative, or finding for the plaintiff in a lawsuit but refusing to give him judgment. This asymmetry even conflicts with notions such as 'fair play' and giving 'the other side of the argument' because these notions are, surely, part of the crude binary vision of most British public affairs and may be seen as the clothing which makes that vision respectable. Linked with this matter of people's mental models is the psychological satisfaction of doing a proper job when serving on a jury – which means judging the truth. To sit for days, even weeks, in a jury box and decide in the end that you should acquit a person because you consider him fifty-five per cent but not, say, sixty-six per cent likely to be guilty would appeal to only the most dispassionate and academic type of mind. Further, if you think, on balance, that a person did do a serious crime, is it not your duty to say so in order that society is protected by having him found guilty and dealt with?

As I went home from the trial, I thought along these lines. Ego was involved. I had started as one of nine and had ended as one of two. I also pondered these questions of how jurors may see their duty differently from the precepts and injunctions of Bench and Bar. But another matter was in my mind even more.

In the course of sentencing Dick, the judge had referred to the probation officer's Social Report. The truth was there all along. Perhaps the thousands of pounds spent on the trial had been wasted. Dick had told the probation officer before the trial that he had indeed been part of Tom's plan. He had lied with consummate skill in his 'verbal' and under very tough cross-examination by a prosecuting counsel who seemed convinced that he was lying and determined to crack him. In my view, he had failed to crack him. But Dick was guilty. The foreman and those jurors who had gone over to him were right. I and my loyal lady were wrong. Having lost the form of the juror's function – the argument – I now learned that I'd lost the substance – judgment of the truth. It was a good thing that I'd not persuaded the jury to be fooled by Dick, as he'd fooled me. He had indeed known exactly what he was doing. Had I?

If weighing the evidence in the special scale pans of 'beyond a reasonable doubt' was our jurors' job, then I reckoned that I'd done it and the majority had not. In my view they had convicted Dick on a mere balance of evidence, strongly laced with personal feeling against the defendant. They had wilfully ignored the repeated instructions of the judge on the burden of proof. But they were right on the facts and their action prevented a guilty blackmailer from going unpunished.

I had opposed, under N.C.C.L. persuasion, the introduction of the majority verdict system by Roy Jenkins. It seemed a major and rash innovation, ostensibly to deal with a very localized problem of intimidation of jurors in a few gangland cases in London. And now, but for the majority verdict system, I would have insisted on my view and a guilty blackmailer would have been found not guilty.

It's not surprising that juries' failures to do as they're told about the burden and balance of proof are overlooked by judges, lawyers and Parliament. If it was a suddenly easily understandable and acceptable precept which all jurors acted upon, the conviction rate would, presumably, drop sharply and the police would become even more concerned than they are already. I have no knowledge of what they say about this among themselves, but I would speculate that judges and counsel go on explaining the virtue of the 'proof beyond a reasonable doubt' to juries with the same expectation that they will be heeded as the priest who regularly warns his flock against sin. Indeed, if either juries or congregations suddenly took heed, there would be complications for police and the courts in the one case as for priests and the confessionals in the other. But as either development is unlikely, it is safe for them to go on saying it. 'A man is presumed innocent until proved guilty beyond a reasonable doubt.' They know what they're doing.

Jeremy Brooks

My summons for jury service named a date which was something more than inconvenient: the week in which a multi-media art exhibition which my wife had been preparing for seven years was to open in London. It was unthinkable that my services, as labourer, driver, technician and moral support, should be totally withdrawn over the crucial run-up days. My impassioned plea to the Jury Summoning Officer to be excused service on this occasion met with polite acceptance, and I thought it unlikely that my name would float to the surface again for another twenty years or so. But I was wrong. Once you've been fingered, it seems, there's no escape. Within eight weeks I had been summoned again.

The experience of others had warned me that the most notable feature of jury service is the amount of time one spends hanging around doing nothing. That suited me: there's nothing I like better than having nothing to do in a situation which effectively prevents me from getting on with the things I ought to be doing. I armed myself with A. J. Ayer's newly published *The Central Questions of Philosophy*, a thriller, several magazines and a notebook. Although I continued to carry them, as a sort of security against possible boredom, in the event both books remained unopened. I found the unfamiliar scene at the courts too interesting to want to lose myself in a book; and any time not spent in chatting up my fellow jurors was devoted to keeping, in the notebook, an undisciplined sort of journal.

In transcribing this journal I have altered names and circumstantial detail so as to avoid positive identification of the cases; but patterns of behaviour remain strictly parallel with the facts, and all general observations are exactly as noted at the time.

First day

Called for nine-fifteen to Crown Court, Newington Causeway. Outside Borough tube station I asked the way of a middle-aged Hampstead intellectual – positive identification soon confirmed – who turned out to be himself a first-time juror. He said he knew the way to the court, having arrived early and inquired in the café where he had eaten breakfast. We set off together through strange streets, making the kind of reserved conversation which ocean liner passengers exchange at the start of a voyage – everyone fearful of being stuck for the rest of the passage with a bore. We were soon lost, and asked the way of a succession of people who all turned out to be strangers in the district themselves.

Arriving late, we were ushered into the back of an overcrowded court, and craned over the heads of a standing crowd to see a bewigged lawyer addressing about 250 passive and bemused jurors. Couldn't hear what he was saying, but from what scraps I caught it sounded like a direct repeat of our written instructions. Jurors were then called by name in blocks of eighteen and assigned to different courts. My block, the eighth, was told to wait 'upstairs' – a gallery overlooking the central hall, with snack-bar and dining room adjoining. Two cups of coffee later, at eleven-thirty, we're still waiting.

Around noon someone must have remonstrated: my block was shepherded into the snack-bar and given a good-humoured, but firm, lecture by an usher on the virtues of patience. 'Bring your knitting, madam. You are at the disposal of the court. If you don't know what patience is now, you will by the time you've finished.' Laughter, and a general air of relaxation. The usher's speech was well-timed. Earlier it would scarcely have been listened to; but now, with a couple of hours waiting behind us, it was just the reassurance we needed: if this is what it's going to be like most of the time, okay – just so long as we know. I hadn't realized how much tension our group had generated, until the usher came and dissipated it.

Nothing at all in the morning. An hour for lunch – I found a quiet pub and scribbled in this journal – and then we were called for the first jury of the afternoon. I was glad to be among the twelve called to sit on the case, rather than among the six reserves assigned to the cross benches. Swearing in – I am the only juror to affirm. Some of the others look surprised, perhaps unaware that this option was open to them: or do they think I'm making an unnecessary exhibition of myself? And did I just imagine that counsel glanced at each other significantly?

Item: five of these jurors could not read the oath without verbal prompting from the usher.

The Recorder is a distinguished looking man with meticulous, gentle, but rather *de haut en bas* good manners; a slightly over-charming man. Counsel are both young: defence is tall, smooth and mellifluous; prosecution is short, bespectacled, florid, pompous. I think of him as Toad. The Recorder lectures us gently but firmly on our duties, but no mention, now or later, of our rights.

The defendant is an obvious prostitute: very pale make-up, floppy-brimmed hat, generous lips now tightly compressed, and a little pinched frown. Prosecution's case, presented exclusively through the evidence of a uniformed police sergeant, who – with the Recorder's formal permission – frequently consults his notebook, is seeking to prove something more serious than mere soliciting: an attempt to obtain money by false pretences.

The officer, on patrol in Mayfair in plain clothes, observed the girl, Pat, pick up a man and go through various manoeuvres – precise in detail but vague in significance – which led him to suspect her of having taken money from the man before sending him off to keep a rendezvous which she had no intention of keeping herself. When the man left her – waving to her as he turned the corner of the street – the officer allowed himself to be picked up. He represented himself as a sailor, just arrived from Portsmouth after months at sea. Pat, claiming to have a flat in Shepherd's Market, said that if he would give her £2 deposit against a £6 hour at the flat, she would tell him the address and meet him there in twenty minutes. The officer now revealed that he was a policeman. 'I don't go with cops,' Pat was alleged to have said. She then ran off down the street, with the officer in pursuit, and, after turning into the Lounge Bar of a pub, was arrested. According to the officer she then made a complicated, formally-worded, self-incriminating statement, which the officer wrote down in his notebook 'from memory' when he got back to the police station.

Pat, called to the witness stand, had a completely different story. She didn't deny her profession, nor that she had picked up the officer. She didn't have a flat in Shepherd's Market and hadn't claimed to: she had told the officer, she said, that she would take him to a hotel near Paddington. She had not asked him for 'a deposit' but had asked him if he could afford a taxi. She would have gone with him, she said, if he had not told her he was a policeman. As to the man she had 'picked up' earlier, he had simply been a friend, a waiter in a near-by restaurant. She had walked, not run, towards the pub, and if the policeman had followed her, she had not noticed. She had drunk a gin and tonic in the pub and was leaving when the officer, with two uniformed constables in tow, had turned up, charged and arrested her. She had, she said, made no statement of any kind: 'I never talk to the police.'

Toad, questioning her, attempted to make something out of the fact that she had called no witnesses, although a 'colleague' of hers had been operating in the same street and must have observed some of the comings and goings. And what about her, ha-ha, 'friend', the, ha-ha, 'waiter'? Pat just shrugged, and gave a wintry, resigned little smile, as much as to say: 'You know as well as I do that we never get our friends mixed up in it when we're busted.' It was clear from the Recorder's impatience with this line of questioning that he found it as artificial as she did.

The court rose at four-fifteen, after a lengthy warning from the Recorder that the jury should not discuss the case with anyone else, including their families. I wonder how many jurors observe this warning. Certainly I didn't. At dinner tonight I gave an account of the case, rather more detailed than the one above.

'Did the copper hand over any money in advance?' asked Margy (my daughter) sharply.

'No.'

'Well, he's got no case then, has he? He's just trying to be smart. I hope you'll throw it out.'

I said I hoped we would, too.

Item: pressure of work on the courts is so great that while one jury is debating its verdict in the jury room, a second case is starting, in front of the same judge, in the same court room. This case is then interrupted whilst the first jury returns to deliver its verdict – or to declare its inability to reach one. The second jury thus has to sit through the concluding details of the first trial. This happened to us today, and I hate to think of the confusion it must have caused in the minds of some of our less bright jurors.

Second day
Court sat at ten-thirty. I had given the usher a couple of written questions to hand up to the Recorder. One was to do with the difference, as evidence, between a written and signed statement and a 'verbal' statement which exists only in a policeman's notebook; the other an even more naive question about rights of arrest by plain-clothes police. I knew the answers to both, but wanted the points underlined by 'authority' to save myself having to make them in the jury room. The Recorder, opening the proceedings with the words 'The jury has asked . . . ', fixed me with a quizzical eye and tilted his head on one side. Like an idiot, I nodded, and was immediately furious with myself when I saw his satisfied little smile. I was dressed like a ragamuffin, but he'd sussed me out: how I hated him! However, he dealt very properly, and at length, with both questions, which in the end came in useful.

Counsel made their closing speeches, Toad almost apoplectic with indignation about the moral bankruptcy of Pat, defence loftily humorous about the yawning holes in the prosecution's case. The Recorder summed up, very fairly and comprehensively, making it abundantly clear that he thought the prosecution's case very shaky, and reiterating, several times, the point that the burden of proof lies on the prosecution, and that if there is any reasonable doubt that the case is proved, we must acquit.

In the jury room there is first the comedy of electing a foreman. After the initial joshing – 'youngest lady present' etc. – the first serious attempt to draft someone was made on me. 'Ought to be somebody who understands the long words – that'd be you, I reckon!' I declined firmly on the grounds – rather too speedily accepted, I thought – that I wasn't respectable. I thought that, as foreman, I'd be obliged to 'hold the middle' in argument, whereas I knew that I wanted to be vigorously partisan. In the event, I was wrong: I'd have been far better off, from the point of view of controlling the direction of discussion, and leaning on the waverers, if I'd been in the chair. A quiet, vague young man with a beard was eventually elected: a bad choice, since he proved unable to complete a sentence or a thought.

A show of hands: seven for acquittal, four for conviction, one fence-sitter. Two of the four women jurors were for conviction, seemingly on the grounds that Pat was 'obviously on the game' and therefore *ought to be* found guilty, to punish her for her sins. The fence-sitter was also a woman. It was hardly surprising that she could reach no firm conclusion, since she was convinced that there was also a man being charged with an offence, though she 'couldn't quite place him' in his relationship to Pat. It turned out that she was thinking of the accused in the case previous to ours, who had briefly appeared in the dock when 'his' jury returned to report their failure to reach a unanimous verdict. Oh yes, our lady juror said, when the mystery was unravelled, she quite understood that there were two trials going on, but she thought that we had to bring in a verdict on both of them. She was quite undisturbed by the extent to which she had misunderstood what was happening and the way the various elements passing before her didn't fit together to make a coherent whole. I would say that for her, and many like her, not many things *do* fit in her daily experience of life, so she's used to it.

The foreman had, unfortunately, raised his hand, rather waveringly, in favour of conviction, and having done so was embarrassingly stuck with it. The reasons given by most of those who were for acquittal had to do, oddly, with points of evidence which I considered irrelevant – certainly not useful debating points. But there was one young man, a building worker of not more than twenty, whose mind was firm, clear and humorous. 'The cop just wanted something better in his record than another soliciting charge. He made up a story, that's all, and a bloody lousy story it is.' Together we took our opponents one by one, questioning their personal reasoning, hammering home 'reasonable doubt' whenever we saw a chink to get that lever in. The foreman was no problem – I knew he'd come over if I could offer him something with which to salvage his *amour propre,* and in the end he found it for himself in a detail I'd been saving up: 'No, but what *does* bother me is him chasing her all that way, and not catching her. I don't understand that, I must admit.' 'Yeah, well, he wasn't chasing her, was he?' said my young ally. 'He went off to meet his mates and cook up the story, didn't he?' Collapse of foreman, and we were left with one implacable lady who was convinced that the officer *knew* what Pat was up to, and that, whether the case were proved or not, one couldn't take a prostitute's word against a policeman's. Only the generalized fury of the jury at the thought of failing to reach a unanimous verdict by lunchtime overwhelmed her conviction: she knew – because I firmly told her – that if we returned without one we'd be condemned to another hour and a half in the airless, comfortless jury room before being allowed to return a majority verdict.

Back in the court, Pat was chewing gum furiously; she looked resigned to what she thought the inevitable verdict. When our foreman pronounced her Not Guilty she collapsed over the edge of the dock for a moment. The officer stiffened, and raked us with contemptuous eyes. As we filed out of the court room the young building worker, my ally of the jury room, whispered to me: 'I wouldn't like to get nicked by *that* bastard while he can still remember my face. He'd put the boot in all of us if he got the chance.'

Fourth day

Nothing for me yesterday, and so far nothing today. I was 'called' several times, but each time was not among the twelve empanelled as a jury. The jury bailiff clearly understands the dangers of boredom, since he often sends an unemployed group to sit in on a trial as observers, just to give them something to do. Some jurors – particularly those who cannot, apparently, read even a newspaper – are pleased to be distracted in this way; others – particularly the heavy smokers, myself among them – are not. I spent much of yesterday listening to a series of boring appeals in which the dialogue between judge and counsel was so technical as to be almost incomprehensible. I'd have been happier sitting in the canteen, chatting, perhaps, to that 'Hampstead intellectual' I met on the first day, who turns out to be a 'China-watcher' with extensive experience of the country. I offer him anecdotes about Russian revolutionary leaders in exchange for his anecdotes about Chinese communes; we're both showing off, of course, but to our mutual entertainment.

Item: in one court where I was sent to cool my heels this morning a witness was asked, apropos the villian she was about to give evidence against, whether he was in court. She looked slowly and carefully round the room, examining the faces even of counsel, passed over the man in the dock and finally alighted, quite firmly, upon the foreman of the jury as the naughty man who had flashed at her on Wimbledon Common. I have a very strong impression that the fog which obscures the minds of a large proportion of the general public is insufficiently allowed for in the scenarios of these courts. The people who make and administer the laws seem not to have allowed for the fact that many people simply don't know what's going on around them outside the limited compass of their private lives; and that many, all likely to be called as jurors, are quite incapable of distinguishing between likelihood and unlikelihood, between fact and conjecture, even, sometimes, between one named individual and another. They rely on Authority to tell them what to think about matters in which they have no experience, and when two representatives of Authority, wearing identical wigs and gowns and speaking with equal certainty, tell them to think two utterly opposed things, their minds, unable to cope with the conflict, simply shut up shop for the day. Every group I've been with so far has had in it three or more people who are, to all intents and purposes, inoperative in this way.

Item: I've heard several complaints, particularly during the first couple of days, that the cards on which the jurors' names are written are not shuffled by the bailiff before he calls his panels together, with the result that one tends to find oneself always among the same, or a slightly modified, group of people. This is to some extent socially comforting, but several people have expressed to me a vague feeling of unease about it. Such groups tend very quickly to develop their own polarities, which are not in the interests of justice in the jury room. Loyalties grow up between individuals, leaders emerge, and what ought to be open minds become clouded by the surprisingly strong personal relationships which rapidly develop inside groups which find themselves thrown together through several separate episodes of court life. I don't know whether or not there is an administrative reason for this lack of shuffling, but seriously doubt that there could be such a compelling one as to override the interests of impartiality among jurors.

Seventh day

Annoyingly, on what would have been my last day of service, with nothing of much interest having happened since I last wrote these notes, I've now been empanelled a juror on a complicated case which looks as if it could last another two or three days. Irritation is somewhat balanced, though, by the interest of the case.

There are six defendants; four young men, two young women – the girls married to two of the men. My heart sank when I heard that the first charge was one of conspiracy, since these blanket charges are so vague and carry such potentially heavy penalties. If the prosecution had any case at all, I felt that it would be all too easy to convince the jury that they were all mixed up in it and therefore involved in 'conspiracy'. The subsidiary charges – of being in possession of prohibited drugs with intent to sell them for profit, or just simple 'possession' – were obviously the prosecution's fall-back in case they failed to make the conspiracy charges stick.

Initial presentation of evidence was very complex, with much to-ing and fro-ing of the accused on foot, in cars, by taxi, and much manoeuvring on the part of the police. Because of the indirect, piece-by-piece method of bringing forward these events it was some time before I could start to form any coherent and believable pattern, and I was quite sure that my rather dour, mostly elderly, largely under-educated fellow jurors were going to have a tough time making head or tail of it. Sure enough, when the court rose with the prosecution's marshalling of evidence still incomplete, I could tell from the jurors' self-protective jesting that their heads, like mine, were whirling. I decided to keep detailed notes.

The facts so far (highly simplified): At the centre of events is the long-haired young man called Watson, whose house in Islington was under police observation for two days. During this time it was visited, several times, by a pale, frightened boy called Jones driving a green (but according to one police witness, white) Simca; and by a bearded young man called Johnson, driving a black Austin. An unidentified pedestrian, carrying a plastic bag, also visits the house, leaves without the bag. Watson himself on one occasion leaves the house and is driven off by Jones in the Simca, returning later with another bag. On the second evening the Simca arrives bringing Bailey, a thin blond boy; he goes into the house, stays for ten minutes, comes out with a bag and is driven away. This is where the first police action starts. The car stops outside Jones's flat; both men go into the flat, come out after three minutes, get back into the car, and are then approached by two uniformed police. Bailey leaps out of the car and runs, throwing the bag over a wall. He is chased and brought down by one of the policemen. Jones stays where he is, and is arrested. His wife comes down to see what's going on, asks at first to go to the police station with her husband, but then says she can't leave the children without a baby-sitter, goes back to the flat. The bag, of which Bailey tries to deny all knowledge, contained 3½ lbs of leaf marijuana and 10 ounces of cannabis resin.

Meanwhile Johnson, in the black Austin, has also been stopped and arrested, a bag with 6½ ounces of cannabis resin stuffed under his driving seat. An hour later the police arrive at Watson's house. There is no reply to their knocking, so they break the door down, and find, in the kitchen, Watson, his girl Brenda and Jenny Jones – who had arrived shortly before the police. A search of the house reveals a wallet containing £1,500, a sealed plastic bag containing 5½ lbs of leaf marijuana stuffed round the U-bend of the W.C., and some torn scraps of paper floating in the pan. More scraps are found in Brenda's handbag. Assembled, these scraps make up four sheets of paper on which various names, times and telephone numbers are scribbled.

It doesn't look too good for any of them.

Eighth day

Watson and Johnson have both pleaded guilty to one of the lesser charges. Obviously their defence, seeing no hope of clearing them completely, has persuaded them that their best interest lies in getting out from under the conspiracy charge. The judge instructs the jury to bring in a formal verdict of Guilty in each case. We haven't elected a foreman, and as I happen to be sitting at the right hand end of the front row, I'm required to rise and speak as such. The clerk asks, 'Do you find the defendant Guilty as charged?'

'We do.'

'And is that the verdict of you all?'

A silly question, since we haven't consulted. I look round at my fellow jurors, who mutter and nod, embarrassed to see the law making an ass of itself.

'It is,' I say, very icy and annoyed, feeling a fool at having words put in my mouth in this way.

More evidence from the police, mainly 'verbals' read from their notebooks, and a confused and illiterate signed statement from Bailey. Of her presence in Watson's house after her husband's arrest Jenny Jones says, 'I just came on a visit – I wanted some advice.' There is some confusing, never-to-be-explained evidence from the police about searching the house next door to Watson's, though whose house it was, and whether or not they had a search warrant, is not revealed: that's going to cause some quite irrelevant trouble in the jury room.

During lunch I wrote out a question for the judge asking him whether the conspiracy charge still stood, now that Watson and Johnson were self-convicted of the lesser charge, and, if so, whether we would have to give a verdict on it covering the defendants as a group, or as individuals. But before I had a chance to send the question up it became unnecessary. The judge had seen the way things were going, and had done another deal with counsel. The two girls were clearly only passive participants in their husbands' activities, and no jury would convict them of conspiracy. That left Jones and Bailey, the driver and courier: not much of a conspiracy left. After some technical trading between prosecution and judge, for the record, the jury were required to bring in a verdict of Not Guilty on the two girls. We again went through the ridiculous charade of my pretending to speak on behalf of eleven other people, most of whom hadn't the faintest idea what was happening or why, and whom I had certainly not consulted. I knew that many of them were already angry at being thus treated as mindless ciphers, and this time there were definitely hostile mutterings behind me as I stood up, under oath, and told a barefaced lie.

Counsel for Jones and Bailey now presented their defence. By this time, due to conflicting evidence from the police witnesses, I was beginning to see both of them as silly boys, barely, if at all, culpable. Jones claimed he was just a driver, that Watson was just one of many people for whom he drove in his hired Simca (his own car being temporarily out of action), and that his job that evening had been simply to collect Bailey from Euston, take him to Islington, and then drive him back to Euston. He knew Watson only as a useful customer, and didn't inquire into his business. He was absolutely amazed, he said, when Bailey leapt from the car and ran off at the approach of the police.

Bailey's evidence conflicted with the written statement made, he said, when under stress and pressure. He claimed that he was approached, at a Wolverhampton building site where he was attempting to get a job, by a friend of Watson's who offered him £15 to take a package to London and bring another package back – it was urgent, he was told, and anyway couldn't be trusted to the post. He hadn't done anything like it before, but it was only an afternoon and evening's work, and he needed the £15. The reason he ran when the police approached the car, he said, was that he had twigged what was likely to be in the bag when Watson gave it to him, but he was afraid of what they'd do to him if he backed out. I believed him – believed him sufficiently, that is, not to be able to find him guilty. There was a bigger question-mark in my mind about Jones: the way his wife had shot round to Watson's house (having found a baby-sitter pretty smartly?) after she'd seen her husband arrested suggested a more intimate relationship than Jones was claiming. But it was still possible that she had gone there because she knew Jones was working for Watson, who might therefore be able to explain why her husband had been arrested.

I found myself discounting the self-incriminating 'verbals' which police witnesses read from their notebooks. For one thing, they conflicted; for another, they were all totally, vigorously and, in Bailey's case, angrily denied by the defendants; and, for a third, I had come by this time to dislike and distrust all 'evidence' of this kind.

Item: when arrested, say nothing (except to demand basic rights, such as a lawyer) and write down, as soon as possible, everything the police say. Never sign a statement.

Both counsel made poor closing speeches: I could have done better myself, on both sides. The judge, on the other hand, summed up excellently, meticulously marshalling the various comings and goings, placing no more significance on them than they could carry, and giving, by implication, very useful readings of the characters of the two young men. Although he seemed to lean a little towards a Guilty verdict on the fourth charge – that of simple 'possession' – he left the door open for the jury to find otherwise if it believed that the two men only suspected, and did not technically *know*, what they were carrying; and I found that whatever his intentions may have been, he had in fact tipped me towards going for a Not Guilty verdict in both cases. I was very aware that this was giving Jones the benefit of the doubt, but since the doubt existed, it was proper to do so.

In the jury room I was confirmed in my accidentally acquired role as foreman. The show of hands astonished me. Nine of us thought Bailey not guilty; seven of us thought Jones not guilty. Part of my surprise was that I had expected the balance to be more favourable to Jones than to Bailey; but most was that we should have even a thin majority against conviction. I had underestimated the jury's collective intelligence.

With a few exceptions, it was a good jury. Argument was heated and serious. I held back from it to begin with, wanting to suss out motives and attitudes. The exceptions were three obvious, and united, examples of the Youth + Long Hair = Drugs = Permissive Society = Guilty line. I left them to be dealt with by a long-haired thirty-year-old car mechanic with a strong Liverpudlian accent, who claimed never to have touched a drug – including alcohol and nicotine – in his life: 'I bet that's more than you can say!' More difficult were the obstinate ladies who simply went on saying, 'Well, he had the bag – he *had it,* didn't he? He was in *possession* of it! So how can you say . . . ' There was a ridiculous, and tediously long, diversion, started by one of the 'not guilty' party, about the fact that one policeman said the Simca was white, another said it was green. Another juror thought he had detected a discrepancy in the times of the police comings and goings, but fortunately I had it all written down. It was at least an hour and half before we were able to isolate the actual issue: did we think Bailey knew what he was going to carry *before* arriving at Watson's house? Did we think Jones knew Watson well enough to *know* he was dealing in drugs?

As in the previous case, it was necessary to take them one at a time, concentrating on a single juror's worries, getting through to him or her a scenario which was acceptable in that individual's terms. We got a unanimous Not Guilty verdict on Bailey first. There were only three against him, and I was able to deliver a story, well supported from my notes, which sounded convincing because I was convinced. It was the Liverpudlian car mechanic who was passionate for Jones, and made out a very good case for him. He was tenacious and emphatic, wearing people down simply by holding the floor longer than anyone else. He made, I thought, a better impression on the rest of the jury than I was able to do. (I had stupidly admitted, in private, to a juror whom I'd thought sympathetic, to having smoked pot, and to having thought it less harmful than the whisky to which I'm addicted. He couldn't resist bringing it up, and I lost some face.) I kept very quiet until the mechanic had reduced the opposition to one, a stony-faced grocer from Camden Town who said that he would *never* believe that Jones was not fully aware of what Watson was up to. I then pointed out that it didn't matter what he believed, because we had an eleven:one verdict, which would ensure that Jones went free, but that we would have to wait a further hour before the judge would accept a majority verdict; so why not go in now with a unanimous verdict, since the hour of waiting wouldn't change a thing. After a long silence, he agreed.

I wrote the verdicts on a piece of paper, read them aloud, and asked for agreement. Relieved nods all round, except for Stonyface. We hammered on the door of the jury room for some time before an usher released us into the court room. Ridiculously, I found my voice unsteady when I gave our verdicts. There was a lot of pent-up emotion in the air. From the gallery, where long-haired friends of the defendants were gathered, there was a little gasp of astonishment, and something near to a cheer. The judge, I thought, was annoyed with us; prosecuting counsel was poker-faced; I didn't look at the police. Jones and Bailey were embracing each other.

Five minutes later, about to leave the court for the last time, I was approached in the central hall by Jones, Bailey and their girls.

'You did that, didn't you?' said Bailey. 'You swung that, I know you did.'

I said, 'No. You were lucky. You had a very fair jury, and there was just enough doubt to tip it your way.'

'Oh, but listen, man!' said Jones, 'we were really innocent, you know? We were just so fucking *stupid*!'

'I was scared,' said Bailey sombrely. 'I was scared stupid.'

'I always knew that guy Watson was bad news, but I swear I never knew *how* bad! Anyway, thanks, man,' said Jones.

I was embarrassed, and left them as quickly as possible. I had suddenly become convinced that Jones had known, had always known, what Watson was up to; and that, in a technical sense, he should have been found guilty. But I'm glad he wasn't.

Harry Cohen

About seven or eight years ago I entered the jury room at the Old Bailey, convinced that the British jury system was the finest in the world, and that it worked.

Six hours later I emerged, quite horrified, and fearful of at any time being placed at the risk of myself being tried by a jury operating in the way I had just witnessed.

Obviously, a belief so firmly held, and for so long, would require events of real significance to shatter it completely in the short space of six hours. I find it an advantage that the experience occurred seven or eight years ago rather than in the very recent past, because all extraneous and irrelevant detail has long since faded and all that remains stamped clearly on my mind are the things that have real meaning and lasting significance.

We assembled in a large hall – about 150 to 200 people from whom seven juries were to be selected. The first thing I noticed was the large preponderance of males, about eight to one, and the complete absence of any coloured faces and of anyone who could reasonably be described as young. They did not to my mind represent fairly the population of London and the jury on which I later served was composed of twelve men aged between forty-five and fifty-five – ten (including myself) were manual workers and two were salaried employees.

From conversations I had early on it was soon apparent that there was a strong reluctance to serve, the most frequent question being 'Is it possible to be exempted?' As I was very keen to serve, because I am really interested in the functions of the law, this reluctance intrigued me and I asked a few people why they felt this way. The replies were varied – some quite simply felt the fee paid for jury service represented a loss of earnings; some were self-employed and feared that a long trial entailing a lengthy absence would seriously affect their business. Strangely enough, however, the strongest objections I heard were from people whose wages were being made up, who therefore suffered no financial loss and whose jobs were secure – the very ones, in fact, I should have thought would have welcomed this as a diversion from routine. It transpired that these people had a deep-rooted feeling of their inadequacy to deal with a trial of any importance and a resentment that they were being forced to make a decision that would decide whether a man should go to prison or remain free. As one man very succinctly put it to me – 'It shouldn't be left to the likes of us to make decisions of this kind.'

This feeling of inadequacy and unwillingness to serve produced a lack of concentration which became most evident during the trial. Even at that stage the thought crossed my mind that a jury composed of men who were willing to serve would prove more efficient, one volunteer being worth twelve pressed men.

When we had eventually been selected into seven separate juries and told to report at ten o'clock the following morning, I decided just as a matter of interest to go into court as a spectator to hear a case which was already in progress. This turned out to be extremely involved – a case of alleged fraud, forgery, misappropriation of huge sums of money in financial deals in the City. As I now had a personal interest in the ability of a juror to follow a case clearly, I sat there for three hours, quite fascinated, and found it extremely hard – almost impossible – to really follow and evaluate the very intricate flow of questions and answers. Pray Heaven, I thought to myself, that I will not be asked to adjudicate in a case of this kind – they might just as well ask me to pronounce on the merits of a Greek drama played in Greek! Had I known at this stage of the complete inability of my own jury to follow a far less complicated case, I would have been even more perturbed.

The next morning, we filed into the jury box to be sworn in. The foreman of the jury was selected by the simple method of choosing whoever happened to be seated on the extreme right in the front row.

While we waited for the judge, I spoke to the man seated next to me. He seemed rather odd but I didn't think too much of this at the time. However, when it was his turn to read the oath he had extreme difficulty in doing so, stuttering and spluttering. Without wishing to sound unkind, this was clearly not just a case of illiteracy, or nervousness, but indicated that the man was of very low mentality. So apparent was this that the judge, to his credit, very politely and tactfully said to the man, 'You do not seem to be in the best of health, sir, and you are excused and may leave the court.' Imagine my surprise when on the following morning I saw the same man filing into another court as a member of a different jury!

The case on which I served opened. It involved four young white men who, in company with others not in custody, were accused of assaulting coloured men who were stated to have been walking in the street, of causing grievous bodily harm and of throwing a lighted lamp (used for road-repair work) into a house where children were sleeping. As there were more than three people concerned in the disturbance and a neutral observer later testified that she was terrified by what she saw and heard, the alleged offence was described as a riot. The case was rather complex, partly because it concerned four accused persons and partly because the timing of the assaults was clearly divided by an interval of approximately two hours, so that what were subsequently referred to as Stage One and Stage Two had to be considered.

Realizing that the case could be rather long and complicated, I took notes at every sitting, to enable me to follow the course of events more clearly. Pencils and paper were provided for the jurors but no court official advised us that it would be helpful to take notes. It was very noticeable and quite surprising that only one other juror took notes. The remainder, without exception, did not put pencil to paper during the entire course of the trial. At the time I wondered how they could possibly remember the evidence relating to four different people at various stages in a trial lasting several days without taking notes. The simple answer is that they did not – but more of that later.

During the course of the trial the twelve jurymen split into groups, as people usually do. There were four separate groups of three people each, who lunched together and/or arrived and departed from court together. The relevance of this is that when it came to voting or changing the vote, each separate group voted as an entity, no one member of a group ever differing from his mates. This led me to believe that in each group there was a more decisive and dominant person or persons and that what we were getting was not the expression of twelve individual decisions according to each man's own deliberations and conscience, but rather the expression of the more positive minority with the acquiescence of the majority. At the start of the second day of the trial, counsel for one of the defendants submitted that there was no case to answer on behalf of his client. The judge said he was expecting this submission and we left the court for a period. On our return we were told that one defendant was to be dismissed. It had occurred to me during the first day of the trial that there was no concrete evidence offered against this defendant and I was pleased and relieved to find that he was dismissed. I mention this incident because although I have some harsh observations to make about the jury system as I saw it, the other aspects of the law which I saw in operation impressed me most favourably by their fairness and impartiality. So the case drew to a close with the judge's summing-up. Despite the usual carefulness and neutrality, it was abundantly clear, to me at any rate, that his lordship considered the case to be very clearly proven and that the three remaining accused were in his opinion guilty. Naturally, he did not say so outright, but I did not think at the time that there could be any doubt at all in any reasonable man's mind as to exactly where the judge stood and what verdict he hoped and expected we would reach.

The case closed; it was about midday. We did not recess for lunch but were immediately ushered into the jury room. The court attendant brought us tea and sandwiches and we laughingly observed that it seemed as if the authorities did not want us too well fed or comfortable, so that we would not unduly prolong our deliberations. The jury room was very forbidding, with barred windows giving a view of a high blank wall and a solid door locked on the outside. It was by no means a cell, but with sufficient ambience of a prison to act as a grim reminder of the seriousness of our responsibility.

As soon as the court attendant departed, the man standing with his back to the door announced in a loud and impassioned voice that no matter what anyone said or if we stayed there for three weeks, he would never vote Guilty in this case. This announcement was greeted by a stunned silence – a most inauspicious beginning for a rational discussion, I thought, and we all took our seats. The appointed foreman took his seat at the head of the table and his opening remark was, 'Well, what do I have to do now?' From that moment to the very end he took no initiative in controlling the proceedings and only acted on suggestions received from his fellow jurors.

The very first suggestion was that we take an immediate ballot just to see where we all stood. This we did and the result was split right down the middle – six Guilty, six Not Guilty. Discussion started when I asked the man who had so vehemently declared himself why he had taken such a final and uncompromising stand right at the very outset, before anyone else had stated their viewpoint or we had examined the evidence. He replied, 'Well, this case should not be at the Old Bailey in the first place; it was just an ordinary Saturday night punch-up between blacks and whites and I would never be a party to allowing anyone to get three years for a thing like that.' Briefly, I retorted that the choice of venue was not our concern but that of the authorities, and at greater length argued that we had to decide on this case according to the evidence we had heard; that this was our function and the severity or leniency of the verdict was up to the judge. My fellow juror would not accept this at all and I could not escape the impression that he considered it far more his duty to protect the defendants from possible heavy sentences than really to determine whether they were guilty or not.

The discussion was joined by others and it soon became apparent that there was a certain amount of support for his point of view. This was sufficiently disturbing for me to introduce the question I had hoped would not arise, i.e. that of race prejudice. I tentatively put forward the simple question of whether, had the defendants in the case been black and the people attacked white, their evaluation of the seriousness of the case would be the same. They all declared most devoutly that they had no prejudice, one man making the classic remark, 'I've got no racial prejudice whatsoever, but you can't believe a word they say, can you?' By this time, despite all denials, I was convinced that prejudice was playing a very large part in the trial and to me this added a new dimension. It was no longer just a question of a jury's competence but of men being denied the basic protection of the law, for no other reason than the colour of their skin. However, it was best not to pursue this aspect of the case and I left it at that.

Another ballot was taken and it appeared that the mere mention of a possible three-year sentence had made a deep impression on some, because the vote now stood at nine Not Guilty and three Guilty. The three jurors who had changed their votes all belonged to one of the groups I mentioned earlier. At this stage I was rather pleased and relieved when one of the other jurors voting Guilty took up the argument. He was the other one who had taken notes during the trial. He had everything neatly documented because, as he told me afterwards, he had had a lot of experience of taking evidence in military courts during the war. So he started asking questions based on the evidence we had heard with regard to identification, etc. After speaking to quite a few of the jurors he suddenly stopped and looked across the table at me with an expression of blank amazement on his face. It had become painfully obvious that most of the jury had not even remotely followed the case. Some did not even remember the names of the individuals – who was 'X', 'Y' or 'Z'. They certainly did not remember who was connected with Stage One or who with Stage Two, or who with both, nor who had been identified either by one person, by two people or by no one. At this point the juror said it was useless to try to discuss the case in detail if hardly anyone seemed to be aware of the details. In these circumstances I asked the juror sitting next to me how he arrived at his verdict, to which he replied, 'Well, I just got the general impression that they were not guilty and that's good enough for me.'

The main part – in fact almost the whole of the defence – was in the form of an alibi. It was claimed that the accused were at home at the time of the offences and the fathers of two of the accused gave evidence to support this alibi. It was therefore important to find out if the jury considered that the evidence of the two fathers bore the ring of truth or if they were left with the impression that, quite understandably, they were trying to protect their sons. The three Guilty voters said they did not believe them, and two of the Not Guilty voters said they did believe them. The remaining seven jurors responded to the effect that they really couldn't say they believed the evidence but who could blame the fathers – 'I would do the same in their place, wouldn't you?' In addition to this they felt very sorry for parents finding themselves in such an unpleasant predicament. It seemed that on looking at these two men in the witness box the jurors had seen themselves – middle-aged, working-class white fathers, with whom they identified completely – and that they were allowing their sympathy to sway them very strongly against a clear evaluation of the evidence as it was presented. I felt it incumbent upon me to point out that whilst sharing their sympathy for the parents of the accused it was also necessary to feel sorry for the victims of an unprovoked attack, and in any case our verdict should be reached by an impartial appraisal of the facts and not by emotions. How anyone could disbelieve the evidence in support of the alibi, on which the defence rested, and still vote Not Guilty was very hard to understand.

Another ballot was taken, resulting in a small change: nine Not Guilty, two Guilty and one Abstention. The abstainer explained his position. He said he still firmly believed in a Guilty verdict but if it seemed possible to arrive at a unanimous verdict he was not prepared to stand in the way. I should explain here that this was before majority verdicts were introduced; if they had been in operation at that time the case would have ended there and then. This particular juror, although educated and articulate, had up to this point taken only a very small part in the discussion. It was noticeable that there were two main spokesmen for the 'guilty' side and two for the opposite side. The Guilty voter apart from myself, who had earlier tried to go through the evidence methodically and failed, decided to try again. After going through a few salient points he came to the evidence of a lady witness. When he read from his notes what this woman had said, one juror hotly contested what he read and claimed the woman had said the very opposite. An argument ensued and it was decided to go back to the court and ask the judge to clarify this point. We did and the judge referred to his notes, gave us the necessary information and hoped that this would enable us to arrive at a verdict and that it would not take much longer. Not surprisingly, what the judge read from his notes was quite consistent with what had been written down by our note-taking juryman, and the man who relied on his memory was entirely wrong.

We left the court and I thought it all rather a waste of time, because although the point at issue was quite relevant it was not vital enough to make anyone change their minds, and so it proved to be. Walking back to the jury room the other Guilty voter said to me that he wouldn't like to have it on his conscience to vote Not Guilty in a case he considered as clearly proven as this one. This was most reassuring because I felt exactly the same way and it was good to know that someone who appeared to be a rational, fair-minded man was equally sure in his own mind of the correct thing to do. Had this man also abstained and had I been left alone then it would have occurred to me to question whether I was being cranky or unduly obdurate. In retrospect, I am relieved that this situation did not arise because if I had allowed myself to go along with the majority it would have been wrong and after calm reflection I would have regretted it deeply.

Back in the jury room it was evident that the man who had brought up the possibility of a three-year sentence believed in shock tactics because he asked me if I would vote the same way if this was a murder trial. Without hesitation I replied that if it were at all possible I would be even more adamant because I could never be a party to allowing someone literally to get away with murder. The question, however, did intrigue me because the man had insisted that this was not an important case and therefore it was possible in a way to understand that he would disregard so many things just to arrive at the verdict that he very much desired. That he would disregard what I considered to be concrete evidence, even in a charge as serious as murder, was a thought not to be lightly dismissed.

I believe it is commonly assumed that it is not at all important that a jury should understand all the complexities of a trial because even if they are muddled and undecided, the judge in his summing-up will give them a clear lead. In view of the fact that in my opinion the judge had given a very clear lead, I decided to put this to the test by asking the simple question, 'Do you think the judge in his summing-up was indicating a Guilty or a Not Guilty verdict?' Three jurors said Guilty and nine said that the judge was indicating a Not Guilty verdict. I had thought that we had passed the stage where anything about this trial could surprise me further, but this left me speechless. It was enough to convince me that any further argument was a waste of time; there was a thick high wall here which was insurmountable. My feelings must have shown quite clearly on my face because the man sitting beside me put his hand on my shoulder and said kindly, as if to help me in my dilemma, 'Well, the judge did say they were innocent.' When I looked even more blankly amazed at this he continued, 'Well, don't you remember the judge saying that the defendants are innocent until they are proven guilty?'

Resisting a strong desire to bang my head on the wall, I found myself in the ridiculous position of having to point out once more the most elementary things which one always assumes that everyone knows. However, I did point out that it was obligatory under British law for the judge to state that men are innocent until proven guilty and that he did this in every case, but this was hotly contested and they still maintained that the judge was referring specifically to this case.

By this time we had been in the jury room for a few hours and it was not really surprising that we were then recalled to the court, where the judge asked us if it seemed likely that we would shortly arrive at a verdict. When told that there was still a measure of disagreement he looked very annoyed and impatient and, fixing us with a beady eye, proceeded to give us a sharp lecture to the effect that the number of hung juries had shown a marked increase lately which put an intolerable strain on the courts plus greatly increased costs – the only people benefiting being the lawyers – so that it was essential to arrive at a decision. It seemed abundantly clear that his words could have but one interpretation: arrive at a verdict – and any verdict would be better than no verdict at all. This was most unexpected – at least it was by me – because I should have thought that the judge would be the last person to ask a jury to sacrifice principle for the sake of expediency. Admittedly, a case that needed to go for retrial was costly, but under our jury system, when deep divisions did occur, were we expected to provide cut-price justice? It also raised, especially in the type of case with which we were dealing, certain important social questions with which I will deal more fully later.

We returned to the jury room and after a few half-hearted attempts to re-open the discussion it was quite apparent that we had reached stalemate. The judge's exhortations, strong as they were, had no effect – nobody was prepared to shift his position at all; there was really nothing more to say. I thought ruefully of a film I had once seen called *Twelve Angry Men* in which eleven jurors, swayed by prejudice, voted without hesitation that a Puerto Rican boy was guilty of murder although the evidence was only circumstantial, but by sheer force of logical argument and deduction, the twelfth juror convinced them, one by one, until a Not Guilty verdict was reached. But the experience in which I was then participating was real life, not the product of a dream factory. The Old Bailey was a million miles from Hollywood and in any case I am certainly no Henry Fonda.

Six long hours had passed since we started our deliberations (if that is a fair description of the type of conversation that had taken place) and during that period no further refreshment was offered the jurors, not even a cup of tea. We had talked a great deal, there was a certain amount of mental strain, and after all that time in the smoke-filled claustrophobic atmosphere and, I repeat, without even a cup of tea, all the jurors seemed tense, rather irritable and anxious only to get it all over with.

Had we not considered this case to be so important in principle, my Guilty-voting colleague and I might well have succumbed at this point, and I found myself able to understand how this could happen in a large number of cases. It was therefore quite a relief when the judge again called us back into court where we expected another sharp lecture to get on with it and arrive at a verdict. However, on being told that we had still not agreed, the judge made a couple of angry remarks and dismissed us – the case was over.

At least, this case was over, but the matter was far from settled, because a retrial would be necessary. Despite everything the judge had said, another trial involving strain on the courts and further large expenditure of public money would have to take place. It all seemed a terrible waste, but taking into account the sharply contrasting views of this jury, chosen at random as all juries are, it would have been a miracle had any agreement been reached.

So we all went our separate ways – twelve men who had never met before and were unlikely to meet again. However, we were all members of one society and had been entrusted by that society to do a job of work on its behalf. Had we carried out our task conscientiously and efficiently?

First and foremost I must raise the question of race prejudice which undoubtedly existed in this case. It is said that justice should be blind, but in this case the jury saw the colour of men's skins and allowed preconceived ideas and prejudice to sway their approach to the evidence and to their ultimate votes. Whether they approve or not, every juror should realize it is a fact that we are now a multi-racial society and if it is not apparent that equal justice is meted out to everyone who is tried by our courts, then we are steering straight into the storm. The United States is a multi-racial society; they have had their explosions in major cities because certain people feel they have been discriminated against even in the Law Courts, and this lesson should not be lost on us. Consequently, if our juries are going to contribute to this feeling of discrimination by bringing in verdicts which are palpably unjust then we should seriously consider changing the system before it is too late.

The foregoing has no doubt made it clear that I feel strongly about all forms of bigotry and for this reason I told myself before each sitting of the jury to be extra careful not to be a bigot in reverse. By this I simply mean that because I abhor the type of offence which had been committed I must be doubly sure on the evidence submitted that these particular defendants had in fact committed this particular offence, or I would myself be guilty of prejudice. It may sound smug, but I doubt if the Not Guilty-voting jurors ever searched their souls in this way and asked themselves to be absolutely fair to all concerned in the case. To them the issue was quite straightforward. It was a question of loyalties – are you with them or us – and at times I got the impression they considered me a bit of a renegade.

Apart from all this, there were a number of reasons why I emerged from this particular experience with the firm conviction that our jury system should be abolished and something entirely new be put in its place. I have already mentioned my reasons for reaching this conclusion but they are worth repeating. The majority of jurors served reluctantly because they felt inadequate or inept, and these feelings were much more deeply rooted than any considerations of financial loss. The men sitting beside me in the jury box showed, for the most part, the same lack of interest and concentration which one would normally see in boys of absolutely no academic inclination while attending an algebra lesson. Had it been possible to give a test at the end of the hearing, I believe the results would also be very similar. Speaking of tests, the thought occurs to me that if the jury system is to be continued because it represents the views of twelve average men, why not introduce a test to show that the selected jurors have at least something approaching average intelligence? Even if most juries are of average intelligence it could be that a large number are not, which hardly seems fair to the defendants in those cases. It might be argued that anyone wishing to avoid jury service could deliberately fail such a test and my contention is that anyone who would do this for any reason at all is of no real value on a jury anyway. Even the army would not employ a man as a sniper if he deliberately failed a firing test by pretending to have poor sight, for this would show clearly that the man was unwilling to perform the particular duty.

As for taking important decisions, a large number of people who are accustomed to making decisions are exempted anyway, and others who never make important decisions in the course of their normal daily life showed clearly their resentment at being put into the position of having to do so.

On the question of jurors identifying with and thereby showing sympathy for defendants and their relatives, instead of arriving at their decision by logical deduction and careful attention to given facts, is it not true that most ordinary people are not rational thinkers and are likely to be influenced far more by emotion than by reason?

Having said so explicitly what I am against perhaps I should say a few words on what I would put forward to replace our present system. I am inclined to support the proposition that juries should be mixed and much smaller in size. By mixed, I mean half professional lawyers and half ordinary citizens – perhaps three of each. In the event of a tied vote the judge could have the deciding vote and this would eliminate the need for retrial with increased costs, strain on the courts and the ordeal of defendants having to undergo two or more trials for one alleged offence. Maybe this method or any other method devised by people with a great deal more experience and knowledge than myself could have unforeseen snags and prove unworkable in the long run, but I think we should try.

One final conclusion: supporters of our present system claim that twelve ordinary citizens without legal education but with the commonsense of the common man is the best safeguard of justice. This brings to my mind the doctor in Ibsen's *An Enemy of the People* who was trying to maintain a position of truth and integrity against attacks from every faction in society and who said he had made a most startling discovery – that the greatest block on the road to a really civilized society is the ordinary respectable man-in-the-street, what he called 'the solid majority'. Is this conclusion true? Is it relevant to our juries today? Who can be certain? But as my Cockney friends in the army would have said, 'Well, I don't know, mind, but it makes yer fink, don't it?'

Iain Hamilton

The patrol car ripped past me and swung across the road, forcing me to brake hard. My passenger flashed me a look of alarm. Two hefty cops jumped out and loomed over us – one with notebook, pencil and arrogance at the ready. Yes sir, please sir, no way out sir, a fair cop sir.

And so, a fortnight or so later, I presented myself before the juvenile court at Paisley (Renfrewshire, Scotland) to answer the charge of conveying a second person on a vehicle neither built nor adapted for the use of more than one person. Following my ready admission of guilt, a grizzled lady asked me civilly enough if I would promise her never again to carry a chum on the crossbar of my Hercules bicycle (£3.19.9 retail immediately before the outbreak of the European civil war, phase two). My grandfather nudged me. 'Yes, ma'am,' I said eagerly. And that concluded my first encounter with the majesty of the law and the diligence of those who enforce it.

I thought it all slightly silly, but it left an impression. *Dura lex, sed lex.*

My second encounter was more interesting, more melancholy. I had, after a fashion, grown up, by way of service in the Black Watch (during which, as an acting company commander, I had more or less learned to make the punishment fit the crime when the company sergeant-major wheeled the miscreants in before me). In 1945 I was on the editorial staff of the Glasgow *Daily Record.* A capital trial was coming up in the High Court, and my editor thought it an amusing idea to have one of his more literary sort of chaps write something about it. All that I knew of the case was that a certain man of a certain age and a certain address had been charged with the murder, on a certain date at a certain place, of his wife. That was all that anybody was supposed to know. No doubt the regular crime reporters of my own and other Glasgow newspapers knew rather more; but I didn't happen to be on terms with any of them (a close coterie of insiders); and, of course, nothing about the case had been published after the accused had been sent for trial. Had anything other than the bare facts of the charge appeared in print, author, editor, printer and distributor would all have been inside, purging (at length, no doubt) their contempt of court.

What I (suspected of writing poetry) was supposed to do (something very properly beneath the dignity of a genuine Glasgow crime reporter) was to write a vivid 'colour-piece' or 'sketch' of the proceedings in the High Court. It was a task that I undertook with a certain curiosity but no enthusiasm, having formed a po-faced distaste for the gay abandon with which such 'human interest' stories were splashed across acres of grey newsprint. I was, I suppose, somewhat priggish.

The court room was large, lofty and dark brown. It smelled of furniture polish and the sewage floating copiously and gently past on the near-by River Clyde. The judge, a Senator of the College of Justice from distant Edinburgh, was a fearsome splendour of creamy silk and scarlet under a bulky grey wig. Recalling the well-worn tales of the terrors of the Scottish Bench in the late eighteenth and early nineteenth centuries, I imagined that the proceedings might well be punctuated by such judicial interjections as, 'Aye, aye, ye're a clever chiel, but ye'll be nane the waur o hanging!' I studied the jurors – fifteen of them, all men, all solemn and intent – who in turn were studying the panel (Scots for 'accused'), a pitiful product of the horrific Maryhill slums. The clerk read out the indictment, the prosecuting advocate called his first witness, who swore by Almighty God, and as he would answer to God on the Great Day of Judgment, that he would speak the truth, the whole truth, and nothing but the truth; and so the trial began.

There are no opening statements in Scotland by the prosecution or defence. The facts are elicited and questioned before jury, judge and public, step by step, through examination, cross-examination, re-examination. Gradually the pieces of the jigsaw fell into shape. The judge's few interventions had been merely to keep the advocates from dragging their respective cases out at unnecessary length and, more often, to help the barely articulate accused when he was in the witness box. His voice was mild, his manner firm but far from ferocious, and he certainly in no way resembled the monstrous Lord Braxfield on whom Robert Louis Stevenson modelled his *Weir of Hermiston.* Then came the closing speeches for the prosecution and defence, and the judge's crisp summing-up. It was all over in a day. By the end the fifteen jurors had no more doubt than anyone else in court that the man in the dock had taken a hatchet to his wife because he suspected her, rightly or wrongly, of carrying on with others. There was no doubt that the crime had been premeditated. That was that. On went the black cap and the accused was sentenced to be despatched to that other world in which (so we are told) marriage and the trials and torments so frequently associated with it are of no account. I cannot now remember whether (as is likely, Scotland having in effect given up the gallows long before England) the Maryhill murderer's sentence was commuted to life imprisonment.

What was clear to me, at any rate, as I left the court room, was that the trial had been as fair as it had been fast. All the same, how would I have felt had I been a member of that jury, sitting in judgment on a miserable fellow-creature who had committed that one crime of which everyone alive, given the appropriate combination of circumstances, is capable? That was the question I pondered.

The next capital trial I attended showed me the English system (now much modified) in action. Compared with the Scottish, I thought it somewhat obscene.

Once there was an unassuming little man called John George Haigh who made a speciality of befriending elderly widows and spinsters in the kind of Kensington hotel which used to house such lonely persons. Having milked them so far as he could of their money on one pretext or another, he would then lure them to an apartment where he knocked them off, stripped them of such jewellery as they happened to be wearing, and dissolved their corpses in an oil-drum full of a potent acid. Long before he was arrested the newspapers were full of the case, packed with increasingly lurid speculation. At last the police amassed evidence enough to pin a charge on him. The case was heard, at great length, in a Magistrates' Court, and day after day the newspapers regaled their readers with the grisly details. Before he came up for trial at Lewes Assizes before Mr Justice Humphreys (a judge who would have got on not too badly, I thought, with Lord Braxfield), everybody in the country must have been fully conversant with all the bizarre little tricks alleged against John George Haigh. Nobody, I feel pretty sure, was in any doubt that he had actually played them.

But surely he must have had at least one screw permanently loose? Could anyone capable of planning and executing such a series of elaborate homicides be held to be in his right mind?

I was then working in the London office of the (then *Manchester*) *Guardian*, in those days a newspaper with a relatively small but influential circulation which did not devote much space to those juicy crimes which gave the larger public much entertainment. The sub-editors would normally compress the Press Association's report of a sensational murder trial to a modest half-column or so. But the Haigh case had aroused such interest that it was thought prudent to have one of the paper's 'descriptive writers' give some account of the trial. So off I went to Lewes, without much enthusiasm.

The prosecution's opening statement tramped thoroughly over the gruesome ground that the twelve members of the jury, like everyone else in the little court room, already knew only too well. Then Haigh's leading counsel indicated that he was going to call evidence to show that his client was not quite right in the head. During this, and throughout the subsequent proceedings, Haigh sat calmly in the dock doing *Daily Telegraph* crossword-puzzles, and displaying not the slightest interest in what was going on around him. The chief exhibit was the oil-drum in which he had rendered down his elderly ladies. As it was being trundled in, I looked down from the gallery and observed what seemed to be a substantial grey smear around the inside of the drum, a few inches down from the rim – the mortal remains, presumably, of God knows how much sad gentility. At this point Haigh looked up from his crossword-puzzle and spoke to the officer beside him, who then reached into his pocket and handed Haigh an eraser. With this the accused carefully rubbed out a wrong solution, handed the eraser back to the officer, and, his eyes fixed on the puzzle, chewed his pencil thoughtfully. Nor was his interest in the case aroused when the defence's star witness, a distinguished psychiatrist, entered the witness stand and gave evidence to the effect that in his opinion John George Haigh was mentally disturbed, and had been obviously so disturbed for a considerable time.

The psychiatrist's long-winded answers to counsel's questions aroused in the judge a tetchy irritation which he made no attempt whatsoever to conceal. Justice Humphreys's ill-tempered questions and interjections increasingly confused the psychiatrist, who was soon floundering unhappily. The defence's case manifestly collapsed during the judge's summing-up when he directed the jury on the matter of diminished responsibility. M'Naghten's Rule was the criterion: did Haigh know what he was doing at the time when he was doing it, and did he know that what he was doing was wrong? Haigh, according to the psychiatrist's account of his conversations with him, regularly had dreams of a nasty nature, but nothing had been elicited to suggest that he had not been fully aware of the fact that his carefully planned activities were wrong, or at any rate against the law.

The jury, smartly enough, brought in a verdict of Guilty, and, as the judge pronounced sentence of death, Haigh looked up at the gallery with a faint smile creasing his bland and very ordinary countenance.

Had it been a 'fair' trial? Well, it had certainly been proved that Haigh had knocked off one elderly lady and had dissolved her corpse in an oil-drum. (But everyone had known, long before the trial, that an unspecified but certainly large number of others had suffered the same fate at his hands.) There was also no doubt that he had done so for gain. But only for gain? We know all too well the abysmal depths of depravity to which loyalty to a creed, a cause, an ideology can force otherwise decent, dog-loving, family-cherishing, art-fancying individuals. Consider the record of National Socialist Germany's impeccable bureaucracy and its agents. Consider that of the U.S.S.R.'s O.G.P.U./N.K.V.D./K.G.B. We have supped full of horrors, and are likely to go on supping. The earth is enriched by the innumerable corpses of ordinary sane humans slaughtered by other ordinary sane humans inspired by idealism-plus-loyalty. On another level, we know that group-loyalty to a criminal organization, relatively small as in London gangs or relatively immense as in Cosa Nostra, can transform a perfectly sane man into a creature of nightmare. On yet another level, consider the things that have been done during the past six years in Northern Ireland. Sane men have done these things. But the mild monster, John George Haigh, had no loyalty to a cause to inspire him, no idealism to drive him on.

The men who tried him had gone into the jury box with their minds full of what they had already read, day after day, in the newspapers. The prosecution's opening statement had refreshed their memories. If I had been in that jury, would I have been 'unprejudiced'? Could I have put out of my mind all that I read and heard? I think not. Certainly I had not been much impressed by the bungling performance of the psychiatrist; but, on the other hand, it was manifest that he had been thrown by the judge's patent hostility to the very idea that Haigh might not have been quite right in the head, not to mention his lordship's undisguised distaste for Freudian jargon. Also, assuming that Haigh's demeanour during the trial was not a carefully calculated act, was it not clear that Haigh must have been in some real sense deranged? But not by the test of M'Naghten's Rule, for he could scarcely have carried out his ingenious killings and corpse-disposals so efficiently if he had not known what he was up to.

If I had been one of those twelve good men and true, what would I have said in the jury room when the foreman asked for my opinion? M'Naghten's Rule be damned; the fellow's as mad as a hatter and I'm not going to subscribe to a verdict that will lead to judicial murder? Probably not, but I should have felt queasy weeks later when the news of the lunatic's execution was published.

It was not until the summer of 1974 that I learned how immensely different the experience of hearing a trial from the jury box was from that of observing it from the press or public gallery. And that was not all that I learned.

At nine-forty-five in the morning, in a mood of mingled curiosity and irritation, I pushed my way into the multitude crammed into the crowded entrance hall of the Crown Court. I was irritated because, although my absence from my office at the time was a considerable inconvenience to myself and others,

I had thought it injudicious to plead hardship or whatever. My failure a few months earlier to answer a jury summons – I had misread the date on the form – had obliged me to present myself in the well of the court before (or rather, below) his honour and show cause why I should not be fined £100. It was on the morning after the February General Election and I had a hangover. So, according to the friendly usher, had the judge. Crawl, the usher advised me, for he's likely to play merry hell with everybody all day. My sense of guilt was most uncomfortable. The law may be an ass, but it has a majestic kick. In the event the judge accepted my explanation but, to teach me to be more careful in future, fined me £10 with a bleary smile and instructed the clerk to see to it that I was re-summoned.

Irritation dwindled and curiosity grew as I hung about in the hall with several hundred others. After half an hour or so we were shepherded into a large court room where an official ran through (presumably for the benefit of those of us who could not read) the explanations, admonitions and apologies set out in the leaflet issued by the Lord Chancellor's Department with the summons. 'Since it is not always possible to forecast accurately when a particular case will start or how long it will last, persons called for jury service will sometimes find themselves waiting at the court for what may seem to them an unnecessarily long time,' says one of its paragraphs. Quite so. My name did not come out of the hat during that day, which was spent hanging about with the rest of the unemployed pool or panel. '... It is necessary to have a reserve of jurors in attendance because additional jurors are always required to allow for possible illness, challenges etc. ...' I passed the time agreeably enough with an intelligent young labourer for whom jury service came as a welcome holiday with a financial windfall at the end of it (his employer had agreed to pay his wages on the side and certify his claim for loss of earnings). From time to time some of us were summoned by the bailiff and sent off to one or other of the numerous court rooms. At three o'clock we were dismissed. Next morning the young labourer and I were once again in one of the batches instructed to hang about. By lunchtime we were looking with real envy at those who came swarming out of the court rooms. 'When delay occurs, as it occasionally must, the patience and forbearance of jurors is much appreciated.'

After lunch the labourer and I found ourselves at last on a jury, having our responsibilities and duties explained to us yet again by a kindly and courteous judge. It was a sorry little case. In the dock sat a sad and stolid Irishman accused of the theft of a purse. Early one morning a policeman had been called to a house in which he found the Irishman drinking tea in the kitchen together with X and X's landlady, whose purse the Irishman was holding. The prosecution alleged that just before midnight the Irishman had pounced on X in a public park and demanded money in a menacing manner. X, according to this story, had placated the Irishman by saying that he would give him £20 at his lodgings and had then taken him there by a circuitous route, hoping to come across a policeman on the way. To this the defence replied that X (a thin, melancholy and nervous homosexual, whose companion had recently died) had promised the Irishman the sum of £20 and then, after a walk of three-quarters of an hour that need only have taken five minutes, X had thought up a crafty way of getting out of his obligation. As to the purse, said the defence, the Irishman, realizing that the promised £20 would not be forthcoming, had simply picked it up from a table in the kitchen and said that he would hold on to it until X got a taxi for him.

Throughout that afternoon and the following morning the dismal tale unfolded, the contradictions suggesting an abundance of *suppressio veri* on both sides as to what had happened during the three-quarters of an hour spent in back streets and alley-ways. The judge finished his summing-up at twelve-forty-five and sent us into the jury room to try to reach a unanimous verdict. I thought that we would manage that quickly enough – for there was only one rational conclusion to be drawn from the few firm facts elicited during the trial – and so did ten of my fellow-jurors; but, alas, we had elected as foreman a self-important pedant who reminded us ad nauseam that even the temporary appropriation of an object without the owner's consent constituted theft, and that the Irishman must therefore be found guilty. No argument would sway him.

Three hours later the judge called us into the court and, learning that we were not agreed, said that he would accept a majority verdict. So out we went again and after a few minutes came back with a verdict of Not Guilty.

On the way out, we passed the queer in a corridor, leaning against the wall, a desolate figure, and then the Irishman hurried past, relieved no doubt, but also, I suspect, somewhat ashamed (for Holy Mother Church in his native island does not share England's relaxed attitude towards sodomy, whether for love or money). I felt a sense of desolation as I walked out of the grounds with the labourer, and suddenly realized that I felt rather dirty. 'Know something?' said my companion at that very moment. 'I feel kind of dirty.'

The next trial I heard, once again with the labourer for company, dragged on at a snail's pace for five full days. It too was of a sordid nature but had more sinister undertones and possible implications.

In the dock were a man, A, and a woman, B, both black. They were charged with inflicting actual bodily harm on a couple of policemen, and the woman was also charged with the theft of a police whistle, tie and notebook (curious objects to steal). A, a respectable and successful artisan who made use of neither alcohol nor any other drug, had been at a West Indian party. At three in the morning he left it and got into his car with a friend whom he dropped a mile or so away. They were tailed by a car containing two policemen and an Alsatian. When A stopped to drop his friend, the police car stopped too. When he started off again the police car kept on his tail. A few minutes later A pulled in outside a block of flats. The policemen jumped out and came up to him.

According to the police evidence, A then leapt out of his car and assaulted them both, dragging them to the ground, biting, punching and kicking. According to A, one of the policemen had greeted him with, 'Get out, you black monkey!' When A asked why, he was hauled out of the car and manhandled. When he protested, one of the policemen told him to shut his mouth, black monkey, and go and live in the jungle with General Amin. When he attempted to free himself, the other policeman struck him on the knee with his truncheon. The three of them fell to the ground, A shouting for help. One of the policemen, during the fracas, sent out a mayday call on his radio and cars and vans converged from various directions.

When they arrived, B, the black woman, was on the scene.

Hearing A's cries for help, she had hurried down from her fourth-floor apartment in a short nightdress and flimsy dressing-gown, bedroom slippers on her feet. She recognized A as an acquaintance and, according to her, asked the police to desist. According to the police, she hauled them and kicked them. Eventually there were about a dozen policemen on the scene. A was bundled into a van and taken off to the police station, charged, and then admitted to hospital. B was told to clear off, but later in the morning the station sergeant despatched two constables to find her and arrest her on a charge of causing grievous bodily harm.

According to them, they found her by the rubbish chute on the first floor, policeman's tie, whistle and notebook in hand, ready (presumably) to dispose of them. According to B, she had picked these objects up from the gutter after the fracas; and the policemen, she said, had found her in her apartment on the fourth floor. At any rate, they arrested her on a charge of theft (not, as instructed by their superior, inflicting grievous bodily harm) and took her off to the police station (on a cold night in the dead of winter) dressed as she was in a shorty-nighty (no panties beneath it), cotton dressing-gown and bedroom slippers. There, according to B, various policemen made a mock of her as she sat waiting to be charged.

A small case, life in certain parts of London being what it is, and not worth even a paragraph in a local paper. But a smelly case and, trends in our urban society being what they are, an important one. We in the jury box were in no doubt about that; nor, obviously, was the judge who obliged the witnesses to speak slowly enough to enable him to take a full note in longhand, while the shorthand-writer (a pretty blonde) took advantage of the interminable pauses to read a paperback.

I had taken a fairly full note myself, out of journalistic habit, and because of this was made foreman by my fellows, against my own suggestion that in view of one obvious aspect of the case the single West Indian among us might have been a better choice. I went round the table and discovered that with one exception everyone found A and B not guilty on each count. The exception was a lower-middle-class woman from a suburb in which you would be unlikely to find a coloured person. (As for the rest of us, two were middle-middle-class and the rest working-class.) Nothing could shake this good lady from her conviction that English police 'just don't do that sort of thing, do they?'

For four hours, ten of my companions went over every inch of the case, pointing out the innumerable contradictions in the police evidence, filling in the yawning gaps with the obvious inferences. None of them had taken any notes, but they all had at least as good a grasp of the case as I. But the lady wouldn't be budged. At one point she addressed herself, civilly enough, to the West Indian. 'You can't deny', she said, 'that some of your people do give the police an awful lot of trouble.' That was so, he replied dryly, adding that it couldn't be denied that the police sometimes give 'his people' an awful lot of trouble. He described how he had himself been stopped at night on several occasions by police cars – 'and, man, when they said "out" I got out, ready to lick their boots if they wanted, because I surely know what can happen to coloured folk if they answer back.'

In the end I asked the woman if there was any possibility of her changing her mind. 'Sorry,' she said, 'and it's my right to stick to my convictions.' So, immediately after we had been called into court and sent out again, I banged on the door; we filed out and I delivered our majority verdict of Not Guilty.

And that was that.

Dura lex, sed lex; but also, as I had learned from my participation in its due process, it is scrupulously and (to my mild surprise) courteously administered. What struck me even more forcibly was the intense seriousness with which we had all taken our responsibility, the scrupulous care with which even the least educated among us had weighed the evidence, the readiness with which we had all (with the exception of the woman unshakeable in her belief that the English bobby was by definition wonderful and could do no wrong) set aside our preconceptions and, as best we could, sifted out the facts from the scores of thousands of words we had heard.

Both trials had been eminently fair – of that I was in no doubt. But why, I asked myself, had they been conducted in a branch of the High Court? And why had they taken so long, cost so much? In Scotland, I feel sure, a sheriff would have disposed of them both equally fairly in a couple of days.

Ruth Male

When called to serve on a jury my first impulse was to get out of it. I was preparing for degree examinations, and the dates would clash. But friends said it would be an 'experience' – interesting, perhaps exciting even, and I should ask to serve later. The clerk of the court was reasonable when approached to arrange dates to fit in with my other commitments, and I was eventually called to appear at the Old Bailey at ten o'clock one morning during the summer of 1973.

The experience of jury service impressed me sufficiently for me to want to make notes at the close of each day, so that these remarks, while impressionistic, are not based on recollection alone.

The case itself – my single one – was a burglary, everyday and unimportant. Almost certainly there are rational explanations, at least to the legal mind, for what seemed to be mystifying aspects of the case and the way it was conducted. These were not given to me as a jury member, and I cannot say what they are. What I heard at the time bewildered me, and presumably the other members of the jury, and still does.

On arriving at the Old Bailey, I was struck by the fact that among the milling potential jurors waiting about there were almost no women. This surprised me as females make up at least half of the population. An usher whom I asked about this, herself a woman, said something brief about the property qualification.

When I had been allocated to the panel, on which I was the only woman, we were assigned to a rape case. This was in the event postponed, as a woman due to appear in it, whether as victim or witness was not clear, had that morning injured an ankle and was unable to be present. I was distinctly relieved at this, as although not unduly squeamish I feared embarrassment and too much emotional involvement, in the role of statutory woman in which I had been cast. As we were taken by an usher to a waiting room in another building, I could hear men behind me on the stairs commiserating with one another over the loss of opportunity to serve on a juicy case.

The waiting room was very drab, hot and airless; the windows had been blown out in the recent I.R.A. bomb blast and were boarded up. We sat around a table. At first there were not enough chairs, though after a delay some more were brought from another room. Leading off the room were a couple of lavatories, to which as the long morning wore on my male fellows had frequent and sometimes embarrassingly loud recourse. We didn't at this stage speak to one another, but stock was covertly taken. One or two had morning papers: they were the lucky ones, the old hands; some smoked.

In the middle of the morning we were told by our usher that we could go out for tea. We shuffled past the steel counter of a self-service café down the street a bit from the court. One man on the panel told me that he had travelled from a suburb a good way off. He had to be careful, he said. He had very little money and hoped they would pay out our expenses at the end of each day, as he couldn't stand to have his rail fares mount up. He wore sandals and had a foreign accent.

After this break we were a little more relaxed with each other. One of the jurors was a sharp, dashing, David Nivenish sort of man. He read magazines he had brought with him; one seemed to be about flying, another on some aspect of the motor car. He hoped aloud that the case wouldn't go on long as it was interfering with his business in the City. Another was old, the only one recognizably working-class. His clothes were very shabby and his long fingernails were not clean. He smoked a lot, rolling his own cigarettes, wore open-toed, rather childish sandals and didn't join in the short-lived conversations in the waiting room.

At one o'clock we were told to go to lunch, and when to be back. I decided to go home and fetch the draught board and a couple of packs of cards. I needn't have bothered; we had been assigned to a case. With my seventeen companions, some of whom had been hanging about since Wednesday of the previous week, we were shown into Court Six. Our names were called, we answered and filed into the box to be sworn. I was last to be called and found myself in the front of the two rows, farthest from the judge and nearest to the prisoners.

The old man with the shabby suit was next to me and, as the usher moved down the row swearing us in, he grew visibly uneasy, shifting in his seat and clasping and unclasping his big freckled hands in his lap. As the usher reached him and held up the oath, printed in large letters on a thing not unlike a ping-pong bat, I became aware that either he couldn't see the words or he was unable to read them. He stumbled and stammered and fell silent. Oh Jesus, Oh Christ, I could hear him saying to himself softly. The usher asked the judge's permission to read the oath for him. Permission being given and the oath being read, my companion sat down again and became calmer.

We looked around us. The court itself impressed me, inspired awe, and presumably it was meant to. The element of fancy dress, the protocol, the standing up and sitting down to order, all helped to emphasize the separation from ordinary life and the enormity of the offence of simply being in the dock.

The accused looked ordinary enough. They were a Mr Trevor Brown and a Mrs Stockwell. She was a lumpish woman, aged perhaps forty-five, with a plain but not uncomely face, and he was a young man of twenty-five whom I took at first to be her son. Mrs Stockwell's husband, Henry, had pleaded Guilty to a burglary on April 21st – the previous year.

The stolen goods when produced were a little disappointing. The main items were pictures, said to be valuable, though from the distance we saw them they seemed to be painted in brown Windsor soup, glossy with varnish, some with broken frames. That none of them looked much was the general comment of the jury later. Among the exhibits was a box of Tampax (opened and some missing, we were told), and miscellaneous items of clothing and household linen, most of which appeared to be well past their best.

Throughout the trial it was never explained how the accused conveyed these things – plus a television set, a radio, several hundred gramophone records and other items I have now forgotten – from the victim's house to their own. Though we did not know this initially, the woman's husband had been involved in the crime, but had since turned Queen's evidence. He was a Scottish manual labourer who looked physically strong, but on the last day of our service we were told that he had in fact suffered a severe heart attack some months before the offence.

The prosecution led off with evidence from the policemen who made the arrest: the accused were caught red-handed in the Stockwells' house. Brown was spending the night with them, and stolen goods were lying all around the floor. Four police officers gave evidence, each reading precisely the same account from his notebook as the other three. They had on the admission of one of them 'discussed the arrest to see nothing had been left out'. Three of the police wrote up their notes immediately the accused had been taken to the station and charged; the fourth had been called out to another incident. He wrote his on returning to the station – by copying from one of the others I should imagine from the word for word tally achieved by all four, including coverage of complicated movements by them all inside the raided flat: who was with whom in which room, who said what to whom, and so on. Besides the police, also in the flat were the two Stockwells and Brown, plus five children all awakened by the noise, and I dare say milling about, and as like as not crying, though this was not mentioned.

Two of the policemen reported on a whispered conversation heard (from the other side of an area) through a curtained but slightly open window. Both heard the highly suggestive words 'suitcase' and 'pictures'. Neither of them heard a single other word; but both heard these.

Two of the four officers had been transferred to other stations during the year which had passed between the offence and the trial – one to Potters Bar, one to North Kensington. Yet all four had to come to the court, to hang about, and to be taken by both prosecution and defence through identical evidence. The expense, both in financial and in social terms, of having such men absent from their duties attending courts up and down the country must be enormous.

Brown was then put in the box where he told what was almost certainly an untruthful tale of having spent the evening in a pub in the company of friends. He submitted with commendable meekness to a reference to his 'accent' (London working-class), to his being 'very indistinct', and to the usual patronizing legal jokes: ' "On the piss" – a somewhat indelicate expression which I think I may take to mean "out for an evening's drinking" ', and ' "Kipping" – which I believe means "sleeping", my lord'.

This deliberate lack of respect I found offensive, and can only hope the accused didn't perceive it, or mind if he did. The judge himself showed no inclination to be amused; he looked as if he had heard it all before. We jurymen commented among ourselves afterwards that anyone ignorant of the meaning of these not very arcane expressions had no business directing the lives of those who used them.

At one stage, prosecuting counsel asked Brown, 'What connection was there between you, a young man of twenty-five and Henry Stockwell, who is in his middle forties?' Brown answered something like, 'I've known him a long time; I have a great respect for him.' To which counsel responded, 'Oh you have a great respect for him, have you? So much so that you are in the habit of spending the night at his flat, when your own home is only ten minutes' walk away?' I thought perhaps I might be over-sensitive in seeing this as an attempt to attach a homosexual label to the relationship and thus arouse jury antagonism, but at the close of the case a fellow-juror volunteered quite without prompting that he thought this attempt to besmirch had been particularly disgusting, unwarranted by anything in the evidence and having nothing to do with the case.

Throughout all of this giving of evidence, the judge wrote a great deal in a large book. He occasionally asked that evidence be given more slowly or that points be repeated so that he could 'get it down'. Technological visions of tape-recorders, even shorthand-writers, could not be dismissed from the mind. At intervals, he took snuff, after which he blew his nose a good deal. The second day, on his return from lunch which he took in the pub, the dashing aviator remarked that he wished the judge wouldn't pick his nose. 'Nonsense,' I said. 'He's nice; he's just taking snuff.' 'Oh he's nice all right. *And* he's taking snuff. But I tell you he's clearing his hooter.' We must all have been a bit on edge.

Although, as I have said, the police referred constantly to their notebooks, the single defence witness, a mortuary attendant who had in the interim joined the Metropolitan Water Board, had no notes when he supported Brown's alibi by saying that he had been drinking with him all evening in the pub on the night on which the burglary was committed. The prosecution remarked dryly on the excellence of his memory. 'That's what I've come here for, isn't it?' he naively asked. The judge looked up from his writing and laughed shortly, a surprising, faintly shocking sound. The mortuary attendant was tripped up not long afterwards by the prosecution, who had in their possession a statement this witness had made to a solicitor in August 1972.

Mrs Stockwell who, we were told afterwards, was mentally sub-normal, as well as being the mother of five young children, did not give evidence. After she had sat in the dock all Monday afternoon and the morning of Tuesday, we were told on adjourning for lunch that certain submissions would be made by counsel, and when we returned we were instructed to return a verdict of Not Guilty upon her, there being no case for her to answer. This was totally incomprehensible to us, but we did as we were told.

On the evening of the second day things didn't seem to be going well for the remaining accused, Trevor Brown. It wasn't exciting, but trivial and boring. I didn't understand what was going on and suspect very strongly that the accused didn't either. The notion of being arbitrarily set in judgment on a fellow whose personal circumstances I was permitted to know nothing about angered and disturbed me.

On my way home, in the street outside the Old Bailey, I found myself – to my own surprise – in tears. One of my jury companions fell into step with me and, not noticing my distress, made some remark about the case. I turned to face him and he asked, 'Why, whatever's the matter?' I mumbled something incoherent about hating to be a part of ignorant people being shoved about. 'That's nice of you,' he said, and pushed his arm through mine for a few paces. Doubtless my reactions were excessive, or will be thought so. I am not young and have never considered myself as particularly suggestible, but that is how I was affected.

On the Wednesday morning, there were further submissions of the kind that had exonerated Mrs Stockwell. Brown had changed his plea from Not Guilty on all three counts, one of receiving and two of burglary, to a plea of Guilty of receiving; the other two were to remain on the file. No explanation for any of this was given to us, but apparently a horse trade had taken place behind the scenes. We were no longer to be called upon to return a verdict. None of us, we remarked to ourselves afterwards, could understand why we weren't then dismissed to go about our business. We remained to hear the accused's records read, and sentence passed.

Brown's record, while hardly good, was inflated by two offences of 'going equipped' (once by carrying a handkerchief and a penknife). He had been previously convicted of removing a door from a derelict house, and had been fined £25. Defence counsel drew attention to the low intelligence of Stockwell, the labourer who had turned Queen's evidence, as well as to his wife's illiteracy and sub-normality, 'as your lordship could see for yourself as she sat in the dock'. The judge, when passing sentence, made further open reference to these tragic disabilities. This being so, why did the handicapped mother of five children have to spend all this time in the dock? The assumption seemed to be that the uneducated lack normal sensibilities, and are incapable of being wounded by public utterance in their own presence of their social shortcomings, even where the disrespect is quite unintentional, as I am sure it was here.

The sentences were not by any means harsh. The Stockwells weren't punished. Brown – who, it transpired, was already in prison for another offence – had I think eighteen months added to his existing sentence.

So why, since it all came out more or less right in the end, was I left so depressed by it? Firstly, it all seemed theatrical, excessive, overblown, imperial. Secondly, so many arrangements seemed to have been arrived at behind the scenes. I had a powerful impression, from the fact that no reference was ever made to the transport of the stolen goods, that those who actually appeared in the dock had been 'shopped', and in return an accomplice was kept out of it.

At least I didn't have to take a hand in punishing anybody at the end of this imperfectly understood ritual.

John Mellors

It came like a message from another world. I was in a tiny house in an obscure village in the valley of the Hérault, just north of Montpellier, where nobody else but my wife spoke English, and the shepherds' French wasn't all that good, and the asparagus and guinea fowl and red wine were cheap and plentiful and excellent. In pompous legal-regal language I was commanded to serve on a jury at London Quarter Sessions in a little over a month's time. Meanwhile, I was to signify that I had received the order and intended to comply. Because this communication had been posted on to me from my home address in England and the English and/or French postal services had not been at their swiftest, the date by which I was enjoined to notify receipt and acquiescence had already passed. It was hard not to feel a twinge of fear that I might find myself in the dock, not on a jury, if I wasn't careful. I wrote a covering letter to explain why I was replying after the stipulated time, but it seemed a feeble effort in comparison with the florid phrases of the law and the coat of arms with which the phrases were embellished. In my case, these feelings of guilt and awe were only faint and temporary, but it occurred to me to wonder how much more acute and lasting they might have been if I were an accused man receiving a summons from Them (The Law, The Realm, The Sovereign, God?) to appear before a jury of my peers. The law, I thought, was a comforting concept only so long as it was in the background, somehow or other ensuring that my house wasn't taken away from me by force or I myself attacked and beaten when I went about my business, but as soon as one was involved in its workings, even in the sort of role that was supposed to be 'on its side' and to help it function smoothly, it began to seem in some way menacing, not a respecter of persons, but a system which had the power to encroach upon one's freedom and individuality. Already, its long arm had stretched across the Channel and the Cévennes to tap me on the shoulder in Laroque.

There seemed to be about a hundred of us, or slightly more, when we gathered for the first time that Monday morning. Together we formed the 'panel' from which the actual juries of twelve were to be nominated for each trial. There were four separate courts in the building. The composition of the panel was, geographically, roughly a third from the East End, a third from the central area of Wandsworth, and a third from Putney-Barnes-Roehampton. In terms of class, the first third was almost wholly working, the second working and lower-middle, the third lower-middle and middle-middle. I doubt if there were more than five or six women. There were only two coloured men. A few jurors were in their twenties or early thirties, but I should say that the over-forties came to something between sixty and seventy per cent.

Our stint lasted for two weeks, each of five working days. During that period the number of trials and the amount of court-time in which we were involved varied substantially from individual to individual. I was on four trials, which together took up about six of the ten working days. This seemed to be about average. Those who worked less complained more and more bitterly as the fortnight went on that their time was being wasted 'just sitting around doing sweet eff-ay', that court procedure could easily be streamlined and the proceedings start earlier (they rarely began much before half past ten), and that too many jurors had been called for the number of courts. At first, the complaints tended to come only from the self-employed or 'managers', but as the days passed and everyone experienced the tedium of having to hang around and wait, the grumbling became more general. The atmosphere among those who were off-duty was strongly reminiscent of an army barrack-room or canteen. I half expected to hear somebody strike up with 'Why are we waiting?' or 'Nellie Dean'. Fortunately, the weather was dry and hot, so we were able to sit and stroll in the open air in a central courtyard, but I could imagine that in bad weather the overcrowding in the inadequate room inside the building would lead to much more frustration and bad temper.

For my part, I found the off-duty conversations at least as interesting as the trials. It was fascinating to hear people express their attitudes to the law, the police, punishment, and morality in general, and then to observe in the jury room to what extent these attitudes did in fact appear to influence arguments, assertions, opinions and, in the end, verdicts. It also led to some self-examination. How far did my own views and prejudices, most of them unconsidered and certainly unformulated, on such matters as property and trespass, law enforcement and violence, the trustworthiness of the police, retribution and reformation, affect the way I thought and reacted when deliberating and arguing and coming to a decision? Would I, after being a juror, change my mind about the jury system, which up to then I had taken for granted to be as essential an element in democracy as an elected parliament, the right to strike and the freedom of the press? How far did a person's past upbringing and present surroundings predispose him to believe that the Knave was likely or unlikely to have stolen the tarts whatever the evidence? Or should be convicted, or acquitted, whether or not he was thought to have done it? Was there a 'sentence first – verdict afterwards' streak somewhere in every one of us?

I was in court as a juror before I heard any of these off-duty conversations. On the first morning, immediately after the mass roll-call and briefing about times, duties and 'facilities', I was called into one of the courts. The accused had been discovered, with the thinnest of excuses, in an office after most of the staff had left at the end of the day's work. The managing director and his accountant, working late, had found him and called the police, who assumed that he was there with the intention of stealing something. The court proceedings did not take long, and by early afternoon we had been escorted to our room to consider our verdict. As soon as the usher had left us, somebody was quick to suggest that the juror who had been last in through the door should be the foreman. It might have been a daft criterion, but what other did we have? We none of us knew one another in the slightest that first day. And at least we wasted no time and raised no invidious comparisons. As it happened, he turned out be a good foreman. First of all, he asked each of us round the table, before any opinions were expressed, just to say whether we were for a verdict of Guilty or Not Guilty after what we had heard in court. We were eleven Not Guilty and one Guilty. When we were asked to give our reasons for our verdicts, it turned out that most of the eleven, including me, thought that the accused had in fact entered the premises with intent to steal, but that the prosecution's case – and in particular the police evidence – was far from watertight, seemed to have been put together in a slipshod way and was, to quote one juror, 'complacent', as if all they had to do was to come into court and say what they thought and everyone was bound to agree with them. The most forcefully expressed version of this majority view came from a fat, red-faced man in a blue suit and, despite the heat, a sort of collared Fair Isle pullover worn as a shirt: 'Of course 'e done it, 'e's a right villain, probably done 'alf a dozen jobs like this, only this time 'e was rumbled before 'e could get 'is 'ands on anything, you can tell 'e's been in the nick just to look at 'im, but the police were diabolical, they 'aven't sewn it up proper at all, you can't send the poor bugger down on that evidence.' The twelfth man, a young, smartly dressed executive – in his father's firm, he told us, where they'd had a lot of thefts and were getting heartily sick of it – agreed that the evidence was not one hundred per cent convincing, but since we all knew 'in our heart of hearts' that the chap was guilty we shouldn't let him get away with it just for the lack of a few clinching details in the prosecution's case; we mustn't encourage crime. He was not exactly howled down, but certainly argued against most energetically. Sulkily, he changed his mind, or rather agreed to vote Not Guilty with his mouth; quite obviously, he thought the rest of us a lot of weak-kneed liberals, if not reds.

After the accused had been acquitted and we had left the court, the prosecuting counsel came over to where a group of us, the jurors, were standing talking, and said that we had been quite right to find a verdict of Not Guilty on the evidence presented; the case he had had to argue contained far too many holes, but perhaps we would be interested to hear that the man who had been in the dock had been there several times before and had twice been found guilty of similar offences. 'There you are!' said the twelfth man, triumphantly. No we weren't, we said, the barrister himself had just stated that we had been right to acquit. We trooped off for a lukewarm tea from the trolley.

It was about a day and a half before I was on another jury. For most of that time I sat around with other off-duty jurors, talking. The Fair Isle man was free, too. He and several others from the East End were quite definite in their intentions. They were not going to 'shop' anyone who had merely stolen, entered premises with intent to steal, or received stolen goods. 'I mean,' said Fair Isle disarmingly, 'it could be any one of us, couldn't it?' He was a lorry driver, in and out of the docks all day, and his view was that if you could knock something off without much chance of being detected you would be a fool not to have a go. Again, I was reminded of the army. You didn't steal from your mates, but anything belonging to 'Them' was fair game if you could get away with it. The moral principle involved was one of loyalty, which you owed to your comrades not to bosses, rather than any rights of ownership.

The question of violence was raised. Fair Isle and a younger man in his mid-thirties, who had been a boxer and then a bouncer, were quite clear about this, too. Violence to ordinary members of the public, e.g. to occupants of house, flat, office or factory, would, if they thought it proved, lead them to make an exception to their expressed principle and vote a defendant Guilty. There was general agreement among the East End contingent on this point. Then came the question of violence to the police, and views on this were divided. To some, the police were simply the enemy, wearing the enemy's uniform, and should expect to be offered violence; leniency was recommended to any accused who had been violent 'only' to the police. Others, including Fair Isle, jibbed at this. Violence was violence, even to the police, who were only doing their job. If there were no police we'd all get done over, wouldn't we? The question was left unresolved. A middle-class man, shocked by the views expressed, dared to argue that it wasn't for us, the jurors, to let sympathies for the underdog, or any attitudes like that, influence our verdicts at all; we were merely to consider evidence and decide whether a case were proved or not. The East-Enders flatly repeated that part of their own standpoint on which they were generally agreed, and then changed the conversation to gossip about various 'villains' they had known, gangs and their separate 'manors', and pubs which 'belonged' to this or that group of the underworld.

However, in the next three trials in which I was involved I

was unable to detect any sign at all that the exponents of those views (prejudices? heresies?) were trying any less strenuously, or for that matter any less successfully, to establish the truth than jurors who took the more orthodox line about impartiality. I could not even look back to the first day's trial and say that Fair Isle had been expressing his prejudices then; he may well have been glad to have come to the conclusion that he did, but it was the same conclusion at which another ten of his colleagues had arrived. The obvious prejudice on that jury had been the twelfth man's 'Off with his head!' attitude, and at least he had expressed his opinions and preconceptions perfectly frankly – before abandoning them.

What did become apparent in two of the next three trials was a difficulty on the part of several jurors in comprehending what was meant by 'reasonable doubt'. It was so far misinterpreted in one instance as to lead to the jury's failure to agree, and the judge had to order a retrial. The defendant was a schoolgirl, caught redhanded by a store detective or 'security officer' with a garment unpaid for when she left a store, where she had been trying on various clothes but had bought nothing. The prosecution's case seemed to most of us to be just about cast-iron. We were sorry for the girl, who wept in the dock and had, we all thought, acted on impulse. The judge in his summing-up went as far as he could to give us 'a nod and a wink' and imply that if she were found guilty she would be dealt with leniently and we need not worry about letting her in for a harsh sentence. Nevertheless, in the jury room one man reacted to the concept of 'reasonable doubt' as if it were a challenge to his ingenuity. It meant, he insisted, that we were to see if we could think of any possible alternative explanation of events, and he could – somebody had 'planted' the garment in the girl's bag. It was pointed out to him that even the defence had not put forward this explanation. That didn't matter, he said, perhaps they hadn't thought of it. There MUST be reasonable doubt if you could construct another theory; after all, it wasn't physically impossible, was it? It was now pointed out to him that although it wasn't physically impossible, his explanation was not based on a single scrap of evidence. Who did he think had done the 'planting', the store detective? 'A person or persons unknown,' said the odd man out, proudly. He could not be shaken. He saw himself now, it seemed, in the role of Sherlock Holmes, not of juror. The more the rest of us argued against him and repeated the judge's exposition of 'reasonable doubt' the less reasonable he became. Furthermore, two other jurors now declared that though they didn't altogether believe the 'plant' theory, it showed that other explanations were possible and, since they were so sorry for the girl, they would therefore vote Not Guilty. The rest of us said we were sorry for the girl, too, but we considered that the case against her had been proved to the hilt. The patient foreman tried another tack. Would it not be better for the girl to be found guilty and dealt with leniently, as the judge had as good as promised, than to be left with the worry of waiting to be tried again, perhaps after several months? That didn't work either. It seemed now that 'face' was involved. Perhaps, even, the originator of the 'plant' theory saw himself able, as the night wore on, to increase his support and change a three:nine score into at least ten:two. He was not allowed the time. After we had been 'out' for two hours or so, the judge called us back into court to see how we were getting on and urged us to try hard to reach agreement. After about another hour we were called into court again and on hearing that we were as far from agreement as before the judge ordered a retrial at some time unspecified. The girl sobbed and nearly fainted. It was, I felt, although not technically a miscarriage of justice, certainly the worst possible result from the girl's point of view. She would leave school and start looking for a job with the prospect of another trial hanging over her, a trial in which she would almost certainly be found guilty and in which she might not have the luck to be before so sympathetic a judge.

Could the judge have explained the meaning of 'reasonable doubt' more clearly and so prevented the search for far-fetched theories unsupported by any evidence produced in court? I had thought his explanation admirably clear, but obviously he had not got through to everybody. I suggest that lawyers and laymen should together work out several ways of explaining the concept and then research these explanations to arrive at that which works best among all social classes and degrees of intelligence. That explanation could then be given in printed form to all jurors at the beginning of their stint, read out to them again in court by the judge, and perhaps an indication given as to how it applies to the circumstances of that particular trial. There may, for all I know, be some advice about this in the 'Judges' Rules', but if so it doesn't seem to be all that successful in its effect on juries. I found exactly the same misinterpretation being made in the next trial I was on, by different people, after an explanation by a different judge. It didn't matter in this instance, because we were unanimous in a Not Guilty verdict, but it was disconcerting when again two or three jurors thought that in order to justify the 'reasonable doubts' they had about the prosecution's case they ought to act as if they were detectives in a whodunnit.

My last trial was one in which the defendant, an Irish labourer, was said to have broken a man's jaw in a fight outside a café. He chose to defend himself. The judge did his best to dissuade him from this course, but without success. What impressed me most in the proceedings that followed was the judge's patience in ensuring that he knew exactly what point the defendant thought he was establishing, and that we, the jury, knew it too. This was by no means an easy task of interpretation, since the defendant tended to miss out vital steps in his reasoning and yet be as long-winded as he was illogical. Time after time the judge warned us that we were not to be affected by the technique or style of the accused's conduct of his defence, and that the points the man was seeking to make were just as valid, or invalid, as if they were being made by the most polished barrister. However, there was not much doubt in our deliberations. Unanimously, we found the defendant Guilty. He turned out to have spent a large proportion of his adult life in gaol. The judge remanded him for a medical report.

What, then, were my conclusions, after a fortnight's stint and four trials?

First, to start at the top, the judges. I have always been rather anti-judge. I think that the occupational hazard of the legal profession is pomposity, and one would expect judges, who on the whole have been in the profession longest, to be chronically pompous. Particularly, I have disliked publicity-conscious judges, the sort who, as if to show how far above ordinary mortals they are placed, ask questions like, 'What IS a sausage?' My experience on the jury did not confirm those prejudices. I have to admit that after observing how four trials were conducted (by three judges; I was in the same court twice) I was most favourably impressed by the judges' courtesy, patience, skill and fairness. It did seem, too, that in one trial the judge would have exercised clemency had not the jury's inability to agree forced him to order a retrial. I thought better of judges after this fortnight than before.

Second, the barristers. I did not think that most of those I saw in action were all that clever. A good touchstone, I suppose, is to ask myself how many of them I would have been happy to have had conducting my defence if I had been in the dock. Less than half is the answer. Three out of seven. One of those three would have been one of the two women barristers I saw pleading – not because she was more obviously skilful, but because she seemed more thorough, more concerned for her client than with her own performance, less remote from us twelve laymen sitting there listening and trying to decide how much of what we heard we could believe. Of course, all the barristers in the four trials were relatively junior, and I expect that in a higher court their calibre would be nearer to that of the judges who impressed me. Nevertheless, I ended up thinking less highly of barristers than before I started.

The most important thing about a court is what happens to the defendant, and I cannot think that the court officials – jury, bailiff, usher, clerk of the court – directly affect that. All the same, they contribute to the efficiency of the proceedings, to the atmosphere which prevails and to the temper of all concerned. The ushers did their job admirably; while preserving a certain dignity, they were helpful, affable, genial. If we were 'out' for a long time in the late afternoons they brought what little was available in the way of refreshments and kept us up to date with cricket scores and any other news from the outside world. I took against the jury bailiff. I thought he was the worst type of sergeant-major, relishing his power, such as it was, over intake after intake of recruits. One of the clerks was a pretty, dark-haired, dark-eyed girl; in wig, gown and black tights (or stockings, I couldn't check) she could have become a focus for my sexual fantasies if I had allowed my attention to wander and stopped attending to the evidence.

The defendants? They seemed to get a fair deal in court, certainly from the Bench. It so happened that the barristers with, in my view, the most shortcomings were all prosecuting.

(Is this general, I wonder?) But, of course, it's the jury that convicts or acquits. What sort of a deal did defendants get from us?

My reaction at the end of my jury stint was one of relief. The system had seemed to work well. There are all sorts of reasons why it shouldn't. For example, we all bring to this duty our own special prejudices, political and moral beliefs, weaknesses of intelligence and insight; we have to function as a committee, electing our own chairman, a modus operandi with which many of us are not familiar; we are laymen whose minds and emotions are manipulated by professionals whose job it is to affect our verdict. And yet, as I say, I thought it worked. What do I mean by 'worked'? Well not, of course, that it arrives infallibly at the correct interpretation of the evidence, so that justice is invariably done. However, it does seem to interpret the case correctly most of the time, and on the occasions when it errs it seems to err in the defendant's favour. The result, therefore, is that the guilty have some small but real chance of being acquitted while the innocent are extremely unlikely to be condemned. Which is a reassuring picture, if I have got it right. I must say I was surprised to come to this conclusion. To hear people talk outside the jury room one would expect that there would be much less impartial behaviour inside it. However, I had the strongest of impressions that in our deliberations we were almost all of us honestly trying to arrive at the truth on the basis of what we had heard and seen in court. Where some of us went astray, so that a correct decision was, in my view, not made, was not because of an attitude for or against a certain class of person or a certain category of offence, not because of intentions to support or oppose the police or the law or the capitalist system, but because of a genuine inability to comprehend the concept of 'reasonable doubt'. And it seems to me that it should not be beyond the power of legal and other brains together to devise a form of words that research would show to be capable of clarifying this concept in the minds of all but the most obtuse 'ordinary' men and women. I would be completely opposed to any attempt to get round this difficulty by the application of intelligence- or comprehension-tests to potential jurors. There are many qualities besides what normally is held to be 'intelligence' which help a jury to arrive at a correct verdict – for example, the ability to tell whether a witness is lying or withholding information – and in the deliberations in which I took part it was not necessarily the most intelligent, and certainly not always the best educated or most articulate, who made the most acute and helpful observations. Everyone who is qualified to have a vote should also be liable to be called for jury service.

Someone asked me a short time ago, a year or two after my jury stint, 'Did you enjoy being on a jury?' I thought at first that it was a silly question. What did he mean, 'enjoy'? Was this question of the same order as 'Did you enjoy that film? That book?' But it was, I thought later, a sensible question if it meant 'Where on the scale "enjoyment – indifference – revulsion" do you place the feelings you had when you were on a jury?' I can imagine people being so sympathetic to the human beings in the dock, so convinced that a social if not a legal injustice was being done every time there was a conviction, or even every time someone was put in the dock at all, that they would have loathed every moment of their service. Perhaps partly from insensitivity, partly from a lack (now) of deeply held political views, I would certainly not place my feelings at that end of the scale. Neither were my reactions neutral if that implies sheer indifference to the effects my decisions would have on other men and women. I think I oscillated between enjoyment of a kind, something rather like what is called 'job satisfaction' (when, for example, we chucked out an inadequate case for the prosecution), to dismay in the instance when our failure to perform our function properly (i.e. to agree one way or the other) resulted in a young girl having to live with the fear of another trial for a further period of weeks or months. My feelings were never so far up at the enjoyment end of the scale that I would volunteer, if that were possible, for another stint. But it was by no means such a distasteful experience that, if I were called again for service, I would try to find an excuse to get out of it.

Elwyn Morris

I had been eligible for jury service for many years but had given up hope of being called to serve as the date of my retirement crept closer. It was an experience I very much wanted to have, but I had resigned myself to the fact that the only knowledge I would have of jury service would be gained at second hand. Consequently, when the summons arrived telling me to report at a sitting of the Quarter Session – the last sitting, incidentally, before the establishment of Crown Courts – I was really very pleased.

On the following Monday I arrived in good time at the Law Courts to find about fifty other people who had been similarly summonsed for service. Many of the people were known to me. Some came from the village where I live while others, whom I seemed to know vaguely, came from near-by towns in the valley. It appeared that all the members of the jury lived within a distance of ten miles from where the court was held, which to my mind is a sensible arrangement as it avoids unnecessary travelling time and expenses. We all waited in the huge hall of the Law Courts, which was bitterly cold and draughty.

After about half an hour, an important-looking official of the county council whom I knew slightly appeared and ordered us to answer our names as he called them out. This was done in the best sergeant-major style. We gathered round him in a circle and the variety of responses – 'Present', 'Okay', 'Here', 'Yes' – reminded me of my schooldays, when the register was called. I wondered if it had occurred to this official how much more efficient it would have been if everyone had gone into a room to report. But this would probably have cramped his style.

Once we were duly registered, there was another wait of about fifteen minutes before one of the court ushers took charge. If the county council official had looked important, this man positively excelled. He was short, rather stout and immaculately dressed, with a rich, long growth of silvery grey hair. He strutted along, reminding me of a peacock. In a voice almost as loud as that of the county council official, he ordered us to pay attention and informed us that we would report to his office – the location of which he indicated with an extravagant sweep of his hand – at ten-twenty each day, so that our presence could be recorded.

That done, he disappeared through the swing doors of Court No. 2. After a short time he returned and ordered us all into this court. The prospective jurors flocked in, but this took time as the narrow doors would only allow two to pass in at a time. I was at the very end of the queue. A man in front of me stepped aside to allow three women to enter before him. This act of gallantry obviously met with the disapproval of the usher who shouted, 'Hurry up! Hurry up!' It was the last straw for the man who had stepped aside. He demanded to know who the usher thought he was speaking to, told him that he didn't want to be in the bloody place anyway, and asked the usher to show a little courtesy. For good measure, he reminded him, 'We're not in the bloody army now.' This outburst met with almost universal approval among his fellow jurors. It provided an opportunity for all of us to give vent to the annoyance we felt at being kept waiting around in the cold for so long. There was a marked improvement in the usher's attitude as a result of this angry outburst, too.

When all the jurors had assembled in the court, the county council official called out twenty-four names from his list and cheerfully told the rest of us that we could go home. It was then noon and it struck me that the whole procedure had been a terrible waste of time. Everything could have been accomplished in less than an hour with a little organization.

The following morning I reported promptly at ten-twenty to the usher's office. I was told to wait in the hall as my services would probably be required later. Another usher, an ex-rugby player, showed me a noticeboard on which was posted a list of cases expected to be heard that day. I found this very helpful since it gave the juror some indication of what was going on.

Later, this same usher took us to the jurors' waiting room. This was a long room with the most spartan furnishings. There was a long table, about a dozen chairs and a hard bench on which to sit. I concluded that one would have to have great physical stamina to spend a whole morning there, let alone a whole day. On the table were some old periodicals devoted to horses and gardening – nothing that could pollute the minds of prospective jurors. I wondered where these publications came from. I also asked myself why everything connected with the law had to be so austere. Could it all be designed to discourage people from coming to court? The public gallery, the jury benches, even the body of the court were all provided with hard wooden seats. It seems that only judges and officials of the court are thought to deserve the comfort of padded ones. The women had a waiting room of their own – apparently no mixing of the sexes here – but the room was as barely furnished as the men's, so I understand. I left the unwelcoming waiting room and returned to the main hall, only to be told that once again our services were not required.

The same pattern of waiting idly around only to be sent home, rather like children who have been granted an unexpected half-holiday, was repeated for a further two days. Ruefully I thought of the Gospel of St John – 'Many are called, but few are chosen.' I still fail to understand why a panel of jurors cannot be called in advance and so avoid the terrible waste of time and the inevitable annoyance caused by the endless waiting.

On the Friday morning, I felt confident that my name would be called at last. When my confidence proved to be justified, I felt like running up to the vacant seat on the bench before the county council official had time to change his mind and dismiss me. Actually, I managed to walk sedately to my place, displaying, I hope, the decorum the occasion demanded.

There was an influx of gowned barristers, accompanied by people in ordinary dress who sat dutifully behind them. Later I learned that these were the clerks to the counsels. There was a slight commotion as the central figure in this drama, the defendant, was led into the dock, accompanied by a prison officer who at once made himself comfortable on one of the chairs provided in the dock. The chairman then appeared, accompanied by two lay magistrates. The former seemed rather bored by the proceedings, but his colleagues, judging by the way they looked around at everything, appeared to be thoroughly enjoying their power. The individual swearing in of jurors impressed me very much. It gave an air of solemnity to the occasion and brought home to me at least the very serious responsibility with which we had been entrusted.

The prosecuting counsel, in a clear, well-modulated voice, outlined the charge against the defendant. After he had been speaking for a while, there was a sudden flurry of activity and hurried consultations, culminating in the defending counsel getting to his feet and asking for a short adjournment. This was granted and the jurors were ushered into the jury room. There we waited, wondering what on earth was going on. After a short time, the court usher asked us to take our seats again and we were informed by the chairman that the defendant had changed his plea and that, consequently, we were no longer required. Once again we returned to the main hall where we were discharged until the following Monday morning.

By this time my original interest in serving on a jury had completely disappeared. I presented myself on the Monday morning, already looking forward eagerly to the Friday when the burden of endless waiting would finally be over. However, my name was called and for the second time I found myself a member of a jury. The same procedures were enacted and the prosecuting counsel opened the case. The defendants were two brothers. The charges were, against the elder of the two, of stealing property and of stealing a motor car, and there was a joint charge with his brother of illegally obtaining goods.

It appeared that the elder brother lived with a wealthy man who had gone abroad for a holiday. While he was away, the elder brother stole the property referred to in the first charge and took it away in a van. A neighbour had thought this suspicious and had telephoned the police. On the day the wealthy man was due home, the elder brother was to meet him at the airport and drive him home. Instead, he drove to a holiday resort and then back to the town in which he lived, where he abandoned the car. The joint charge alleged that the brothers had obtained goods to the value of £800 by false pretences.

I had no difficulty at all in following the case made out by the prosecuting counsel. A number of witnesses were called and their cross-examination by defending counsel raised many doubts in my mind. It seemed that everything depended on the question of identity. These doubts were increased by the final submission of defending counsel. The chairman of the Bench then made his summing-up. His address was most helpful, at least as far as I was concerned. He stressed the relevant matters, and instructed us as to what was irrelevant. With regard to the charge of stealing the car, he advised that if we thought the evidence was insufficient to justify a verdict of Guilty, we could consider whether the defendant was guilty of taking away the car without the owner's consent.

With that, we were told to retire to consider our verdict. Having listened intently for about two-and-a-half hours, there was a feeling of intense relief among the jury, and the smokers among us lit up with obvious satisfaction in the jury room.

The jury consisted of three women and nine men. I knew one of the women very well since we live in the same village. She introduced me to the other ladies. One was a quiet, elderly widow from a neighbouring town, while the other, a woman in her late forties who worked in a school canteen, confessed that her only ambition was to get away from the court as quickly as possible. She said to me, almost sorrowfully, 'I hate the police and anything to do with them.' These three immediately secured chairs in a far corner of the room where they sat, their knees almost touching, puffing deeply on their cigarettes.

One man, whom I had not noticed before, started a detailed inspection of the walls of the jury room the moment we entered it. Whether building or decorating was his occupation I was unable to ascertain. However, with the exception of these four, everyone seemed determined to be sociable.

Two men recognized each other and discovered that they had both been at a concert in a working men's club some weeks before. They were joined by a third man who announced that he was a member of the same club. The clubmen, as I called them, took their seats at the table and were loud in their praise of the club and its entertainment. A man whom I knew to be an ex-miner said, 'Let's get on with the bloody thing. I want to get home to go to work tonight.' Mr A, an extravagantly dressed, rather superficial man who had great confidence in his own abilities, suggested that he should act as foreman. No one offered objection or approval. With obvious satisfaction, Mr A took his seat at the head of the table and called on us to get started. The clubmen continued their discussion, while the wall inspector, apparently satisfied with the construction of the walls, was now giving the window a close scrutiny.

Next to Mr A was a handsome man in his mid-fifties whom I shall call Mr B. He was a trade union official, a chapel deacon and the secretary of a local W.E.A. branch. (I found this out in a casual conversation I had with him on a previous day.) He indicated his annoyance at the delay by shaking his head. Then, since Mr A's appeal had met with little success, Mr B politely asked the clubmen to pay attention. The ladies had not moved from their corner, and since I knew one of them I asked her if she and the other two would take their seats at the table. 'Oh you men settle it among yourselves,' she replied and the women took no part and showed no interest at all in what followed.

Mr B suggested that we discuss the first charge, that of stealing property, bearing in mind that, since the alleged offence had been committed in the dark, there was a possibility that the neighbour who had identified the defendant might have been mistaken. One man who had not previously spoken pointed out that this was unlikely because the witness had been very close to the defendant when he was carrying the goods out to the van. The two ex-miners launched into tales of recognition in the dark when they were underground. Some of these incidents bore little or no relation to the point under discussion. Mr B explained that he had raised the point precisely because it had been stressed by the chairman in his summing-up. He suggested that Mr A should put the matter to the jury to see if we agreed. This was met by a loud 'yes' from the ex-miners and one of the clubmen. This excited the interest of the wall inspector, though only temporarily.

The foreman, obviously pleased with this show of approval, moved on to the question of stealing the car. One of the ex-miners felt very strongly about this. 'I've got a car,' he announced, 'and if anyone jumps into it and drives it off, he's stealing it, see?' This forthright contribution made a great impression on two of the clubmen and the other ex-miner. I ventured that since the defendant was living with the plaintiff and was due to drive to the airport to collect him, with his approval, he could hardly have been guilty of stealing the car.

My contribution had little effect. The ex-miner turned to me. 'He took the car, didn't he? He didn't go to the airport, did he? He went to the holiday resort instead, didn't he? Therefore, he stole the car.' I was completely subdued by this rather forceful reasoning. The foreman looked from the ex-miner to me as though wondering if I had the temerity to question such emphatic logic. The foreman was about to move on to the next charge when Mr B said, 'Now, if I was stealing a car, I would not leave it on the roadside in a built-up area where it could easily be seen. I would try to hide the car until I could change the number plates and do everything possible to make recognition difficult. This the defendant didn't do. He merely left it on the roadside where the police could see it, after it had been reported stolen.' I indicated my agreement and reminded them that the chairman had gone out of his way to say that we could consider the lesser charge of driving the car away without the owner's consent.

At this the ex-miner's colleague, obviously feeling a duty to support his friend, said, 'Look here, mate, have you got a car?' I assured him I didn't own one. He turned to Mr B and asked him the same question, and again received a negative reply. 'Well I have, see, and anyone who drove that car would be stealing it,' he said, almost aggressively. Mr B addressed the two ex-miners. 'Now, having stolen the car, what would you have done? Would you have left it at the roadside for everyone to see? No. If you couldn't sell it, you would at least try to hide it and have it resprayed. Now use your heads, boys. All we can do,' he went on quietly, 'is to accept the alternative charge. This fellow is not guilty of stealing the car, but guilty of driving the car away without the owner's consent.'

The quiet reasoning of Mr B had a profound effect on the two ex-miners, and one of the clubmen agreed that there was a lot of sense in this. I suggested that we put it to the vote and when asked if we agreed with Mr B's view, there was a chorus of assent.

Having dispensed with the first two charges, we discussed the third, that of jointly obtaining goods by false pretences. The case depended on whether the men intended paying for the goods and, again, on the question of identity. This was a straightforward case and no one offered any objection to one of the clubmen's view that 'They are, of course, guilty.' One of the men sitting at the top of the table who had hitherto not uttered a word said loudly, 'Thank God the bloody thing's over.' The juror who had been inspecting the walls, apparently having concluded that they were satisfactory, now took a chair and appeared to be wondering what the next step was. One of the ladies sitting in the corner called out, 'Have you finished now?' Everyone seemed pleased that we had come to a decision.

The foreman called for attention and said that when called upon to deliver our verdict, he intended to add that the jury commended the action of the neighbour concerned in the first charge in telephoning the police. 'You see,' he went on, 'there's so much vandalism and selfishness around these days that anyone acting as the witness did deserves to be commended.' There was complete silence for a moment, then one of the clubmen said, 'Do you have to say that?' It looked as though we were in for another long argument. Mr B grimaced and said, almost angrily, 'We are not here to commend or criticize anyone. We are here to decide, on the evidence given, whether these men are guilty or not. If any comments are needed, no doubt the chairman will make them when he passes sentence.'

He spoke with such authority that no one said a word. The foreman was obviously annoyed and went into a bad sulk. Someone shouted, 'Tell them we're ready.' The wall inspector jumped into action, rushed to the door and gave a loud knock. The door was immediately opened by the usher and we filed back into court. The foreman was asked to stand up. He was then asked what our verdict was on each charge. This was Mr A's big moment. He spoke in a loud voice and, on the second charge, added that the defendant was guilty of taking the car away without the consent of the owner.

Listening to the foreman, I could not help thinking how sensible and wise he sounded. No doubt the people sitting in the court thought that our decision was that of twelve sensible people, reached after serious deliberations on the evidence given. In fact, only five people really took part in the deliberations to any purpose. This was a simple, straightforward case. Had it been a complicated one I dread to think what would have gone on in the jury room.

Before sentence was passed, the previous records of the two men were read out. They were not, by any means, model citizens. If I had known this before it would certainly have affected my reaching an unbiased decision. I would have had to remind myself continually that the men were being tried for this particular offence, and my knowledge of their previous convictions would have hindered my ability to be impartial.

We are told that the right to a trial by jury is one of the bulwarks of justice in this country. This is good in theory since it presupposes that everyone is equal. In spite of that, there is quite a strong case to be made for the introduction of a test of ability for jurors. Having said that, the question naturally arises, what would the test be for? Would it be for literacy or for commonsense? If the latter, in what form would the test be given? And by whom? Posing the question actually raises more questions than it solves. I feel that the jury system involves a great deal of luck. We were extremely fortunate in having a man of Mr B's calibre sitting with us and it is probably too much to expect every jury to contain one such able man. I contend, therefore, that the quality of a jury and the decisions arrived at depend entirely on the luck of the draw.

Young people were conspicuous by their absence and at the time I wondered if this was unusual. I fail to see what owning or occupying premises with a rateable value of £x has to do with the ability to serve on a jury. Now that people of eighteen are able to vote, I am glad to learn that they are eligible for jury service. Similarly, it seems to me foolish that a man should be deemed unfit for jury service once he attains the age of sixty, especially when one considers that lay magistrates could (until very recently when they have been compulsorily retired at seventy) continue to adjudicate until they died.

Although the two lay magistrates did not take any active part in the proceedings, I would not suggest that their presence was of no use. Lay magistrates are often people with many years practical magisterial experience, who sit on the Bench of County Magistrates' Courts. They are drawn from a wide section of the community and include a variety of workers. The chairman of a higher court is a trained barrister. In a sense, this combination of lay and legally trained minds makes up a miniature jury, with the crucial difference that the chairman is on hand to assess the case from a legal point of view, while the lay magistrates can advise on social or everyday matters. The great advantage of this system is that it provides for the view of ordinary people and this helps the Bench as a whole to take a more objective and complete view of the case when passing sentence. My own view is that every criminal court should have lay assessors to ensure that Lord Hewart's wise words, 'Justice should not only be done, but manifestly and undoubtedly be seen to be done,' were more frequently put into practice.

From my limited experience, and at the risk of being presumptuous, I think that a jury should be briefly instructed in matters of procedure before hearing a case. This would doubtless seem unnecessary and trite to people who are used to committee work and to those who have served before, but the whole approach should be geared to the needs of those without experience who surely make up the majority called upon to serve. I am sure that it would be very helpful if all jurors received a short talk on court procedure, the appointment of a foreman, the need to discuss each charge individually etc., on the first day of service.

I did not sit on a jury again. Friday came and I collected my travelling expenses and was finally dismissed. For almost twenty years I had looked forward to the opportunity of serving on a jury and when it came the experience proved to consist, in the main, of standing about in draughty corridors, talking to people as bored as I was, until we all seemed to be near complete exasperation.

Jeremy Potter

A jury summons is an intrusion into private life akin to an army call-up. However busy you are, whatever your need to earn a living, you must cancel all engagements for the duration. If you are not in an exempt category your only sure-fire counter-ploy is a medical certificate of incontinence.

The date for which I was summoned fell in the middle of my holiday period. Although the printed form is severely worded, I decided not to be deterred. I wrote that I was due to be abroad on that day and that altering my arrangements would be expensive; that I was not seeking to evade service, but would it be possible to serve at a later date? I did not mention the word 'holiday', but every word I did mention was the truth and nothing but the truth. A printed excusal arrived by return of post. It was followed after three months by a new summons. Full marks to Mr Big for being both humane and efficient.

Full marks too to the jury bailiff who received our mob of about two hundred raw recruits at the London Crown Courts, like a sergeant-major at a regimental depot coping manfully with yet another scruffy intake. We were certainly a nondescript lot and he was stern but just, calling the roll, dividing us into herds of fourteen (more than twelve to allow for objections) and ordering each herd to be shepherded to one of the courts. When this had been accomplished there were plenty of left-overs, and this unembodied contingent was marched to the jury cafeteria.

The session was to last for six weeks and a relief force of other good men and true would replace us at half time. Meanwhile the jury cafeteria was ugly and uncomfortable and it had not occurred to me that jury service would mean imprisonment in such a room for most of the hours of daylight over a period of three weeks. Slipping out for a breath of air would be treated as absence without leave; as desertion, if prolonged. Even instructional visits to the public gallery of one of the courts were not permitted. A case might take an hour or a week and it was the job of the jury bailiff to muster a permanent pool of ever-ready reserves. I would guess that during the three weeks most of us sat on a minimum of three cases and a maximum of six, taking up a total time of between one and two weeks actually spent in one or other of the various courts.

When the courts rose at lunchtime the captive pool was released: 'Back at two o'clock.' The jury restaurant was handy and wholesome, but few chose to stay on the premises. I had asked my secretary for a short list of Cordon Bleu eating places in the neighbourhood of the Elephant and Castle, and the list had proved very short indeed; blank, in fact. However, the local pubs knew the requirements of jurymen. The World's End in Newington Causeway offered lunchtime strip on Mondays, Tuesdays and Wednesdays. On Thursdays and Fridays there was topless go-go dancing at The Hole in the Wall in Borough High Street. It was bubs in the beer and then back at two sharp to look the accused in the eye or sit in the cafeteria until four-thirty or five, when some of us would leave woozy-headed for our offices to start a real day's work.

So much hanging-about emboldened me to ask for compassionate leave. I put in two applications. One was to have lunch with Mr Harold Wilson: permission refused. The second was to attend a board meeting: permission granted. The discrimination had nothing to do, I feel sure, with the jury bailiff's view of the relative importance of Mr Wilson and board meetings. He was concerned only with the current state of play in the courts plus, of course, the overriding need to maintain discipline.

When our names were called and we were led away to a court to do our duty at last, two further hazards had to be overcome. If ours were not among the first twelve names we could find ourselves quickly back in the cafeteria. Alternatively we could be objected to, and this is damaging to the ego. As we take the Bible in our right hand (I am left-handed but have never managed to interest a lawyer in the fact) and prepare to read the solemn formula from the printed card, counsel says

'Object', and we are hustled humiliatingly out of court.

'Why were you objected to?' I asked a reject who returned unexpectedly to his seat beside me in the cafeteria.

'Short hair,' he replied. 'Not that they ever say.'

He was ruffled, but we agreed that if the defendant was long-haired it might be good policy for his counsel to winkle the short-back-and-sides brigade out of the jury box. But the next day I was objected to, and my hair tends to straggle. He consoled me in turn, this time with the thought that if the case against the accused is virtually watertight the only hope is to object to jurors who look intelligent. The theory flattered me but did not prevent my feeling apprehensive when I next took the Bible in my right hand. One rejection was bad enough, two would be past bearing. On this occasion, though, I passed muster.

Empanelled at last and believing that the disruption to my life was now to be justified, I was in for a serious disappointment. The cases with which I was concerned were without exception of the utmost triviality, and this was the general experience. After two days spent in deciding whether someone had taken sixty-five pence from a gas meter or three days deciding whether someone had broken a window in a pub, jurors whose daily lives and livelihoods were suffering while they did their duty as citizens tended to become resentful. They were also very conscious of the cost to public funds. It would be salutary if at the end of such cases the judge were to hold up a card giving an estimated figure so that we could all read in our newspapers that '£5,700 of taxpayers' money was spent yesterday at the London Crown Courts in securing the conviction of Joe Bloggs for breaking a window in a public house.' The public might then ask itself what the country has magistrates for and whether the right to trial by jury should extend quite so far down the line.

These trivial cases cluttering the courts must make a major contribution to the law's most serious blemish: delay. Another factor is the startling fact that many trials are conducted at the speed at which the judge is able to operate a pencil. There is a shorthand-writer too, but the electronic age which has been with us for some years in the outside world has not yet reached the courts. The judge's long-hand is evidently a *sine qua non* of English justice. It is not that he makes a memorandum of crucial or salient points: he seems determined to make the shorthand-writer redundant by taking down every word uttered by every witness. This results in some old police hands appearing to suffer from impediments in their speech. When they declaim from the witness box, 'I was proceeding along . . . the High Street at . . . eleven-thirty p.m. on the evening of . . .' they are only trying to be helpful, keeping an eye on the judge's pencil and going at dictation speed. Surely, though, his lordship would be happier recapturing it all with the aid of a tape-recorder, and justice might then be administered at twice the speed and half the cost.

None of the cases in which I was involved dealt with offences or alleged offences which had taken place less than twelve months previously. (This, incidentally, is a sufficient reason in itself why every motorist accused of an offence which might lose him his licence opts for trial by jury: he can go on driving for at least another year before the case is heard.) The result of this time-gap is to induce a general atmosphere of unreality and disbelief, as though everyone is participating in a Kafka novel. Policemen thumb desperately through their notebooks trying to remember anything at all about what happened in this particular case, and other witnesses under cross-examination swear to details which they cannot possibly remember. I waited in vain for something like this from someone who had sworn to tell the truth: 'Actually, if you really want the truth, it was all so long ago that I can't remember a single blinding thing about it and, what's more, I'm prepared to bet your lordship a fiver that that goes for the accused and all the other witnesses too.'

It is no doubt inevitable that the jury should be taken through the same set of circumstances time and time and time again – by any number of witnesses and by the accused and both counsel – but it was surprising to find the judges repeating it all yet again under the guise of a summing-up. At the end of the trial there was no drawing of the jury's attention to this, that or the other, but simply a full reading of those laboriously written notes. Could this result from the misinterpretation of some instruction about the impropriety of guiding juries, or was the recital simply a substitute for thought? I must record my view that some of the judges at the London Crown Courts were not of a high quality, and the same could be said of some of the barristers. Not all, I hasten to add in fairness and out of fear of defamation. On checking in some other legal circles I was told that County Court judges are paid far less than successful barristers and that barristers' fees at the London Crown Courts were at that time unduly low.

Without having given the matter any previous thought, I found that I could not approve of twentieth-century justice being administered in eighteenth-century dress. The effect of wigs and gowns is to intimidate the layman and confirm his suspicions that the law is hopelessly out of date. Dressing-up for ceremonial occasions is a harmless pastime in a backward-looking country, but fancy dress when a man's liberty is at stake seemed perverse, if not sadistic. Wigs and gowns visibly separate those who are members of the club and know the rules from those who are interlopers and don't. Juries belong to the latter category. They don't qualify for fancy dress and are not told the rules. We learned nothing of our rights – to put questions to the judge, for instance – only our obligations, and these could have done with some clarification.

We had to swear, for example, to try cases on the evidence put in front of us. In practice we might well reach a decision on the basis of the evidence which was not put in front of us, either reading between the lines or drawing deductions from dogs not barking in the night. The most obvious of these cases is when the accused chooses not to go into the witness box and expose himself to cross-examination. There are plenty of others. What is the jury to make of the accused's girlfriend not appearing as a witness to corroborate his statement that they were in bed together at the time when the crime was committed? No explanation is offered by either counsel. Is the jury supposed to erase her non-appearance from their minds? In this connection it is an important consideration from the jury's point of view that neither side is concerned to tell them the truth. Each is presenting a case in which the evidence it produces is selective and tendentious. Neither counsel lies, but in doing his best in accord with his brief he is precluded from dealing in anything so dangerous as the whole truth.

As for the juries themselves, an average membership seemed to consist of eight more or less unremarkable pinko-grey London males, one Irishman, one coloured man, one homosexual and one woman. The Irishman and the coloured man tended, as a matter of principle, not to believe a single word of the police evidence, and the homosexual, too tender-hearted to sit in judgment of his fellow men, could barely face the responsibility of convicting anyone of anything. To overcome this built-in not guilty faction the other nine had to be very sure of themselves if they believed the accused guilty. In the end it was the views of one or two strong-minded members which usually prevailed. Sometimes there was considerable misunderstanding and confusion of thought expressed in the jury room, and the system appeared to me to be saved from total wreck only by the innate sharpwittedness of the average Londoner. Your electrician's mate from Shepherd's Bush tends to know exactly what's what and to be able to judge as accurately as anyone who is lying and who is telling the truth. Just as the proper working of democracy requires a knowledgeable electorate, knowledgeable jurymen are essential if our legal system is to be effective. Illiterate juries in past centuries were doubtless a lot better than no juries at all, but the judge normally made up their minds for them. Today's jurymen have – rightly – to sort matters out for themselves.

Jury*men* is the right word. Despite constant assurances over the years that the matter is being put right, women jurors seem to have remained remarkably scarce. At the London Crown Courts the ration of one per jury appeared to be standard. My own wife is the joint owner of our house, but she did not have a 'J' in the electoral register as I had. Now that being a householder is no longer the qualification, I wonder how long it will be before women achieve equal representation. Once their children are of an age to manage by themselves, they are usually better placed to undertake jury service. Why the authorities should be so chary of them is a mystery to me. A jury dominated by women would, I believe, be more likely to convict than one dominated by men.

As time passed, it became apparent that acquittals were more frequent while jurors were green. If you are an accused you will do well to have your case first on the list. At that stage plenty of jurymen will believe that there is reasonable doubt if no one has actually seen you with your hand in the till. If, after long argument and with several of them still doubtful, they find you guilty and then discover that you have seventeen previous convictions for similar offences, scales tend to drop from their eyes; they become old soldiers overnight and the next accused is viewed much more circumspectly.

By and large I received the impression that many guilty people get away with a verdict of Not Guilty. We are apt to shrug this off as unimportant compared to innocent people being found guilty, but it cannot be unimportant in itself. Whenever it happens justice is not being done. Such a defect in the system is damaging to society and unfair to subsequent victims. If it goes too far, the backlash could be unpleasant. In America a conservative is currently defined as a liberal who has been mugged.

Until we retired to the jury room to consider our verdict we never had a foreman. There was no opportunity to elect one earlier, so that we were without a spokesman while the cases were in progress. Since juries are differently composed for every case we were nearly always strangers and without the means of determining who might do the job well. In the jury room anyone who wanted to be foreman would take the seat at the end of the table and say, 'Well, who's going to be foreman then?' At which someone would obligingly clinch it for him by replying, 'What about you then? You're sitting there. Why don't you do it?'

On one occasion the would-be foreman seemed to be unbalanced and thoroughly unsuitable. Before anyone else could speak I therefore countered his question with a different response. 'What about the wise-looking, grey-haired man?' I said, pointing to someone with whom I had had lunch. 'He would do it admirably.' No one was impolite enough to dissent, and he did do the job admirably. It was a difficult case, we were a disputatious lot, and the other man would have been a disaster. The charge was drunken driving, and this brings out another anti-police faction: the dedicated motorists. At one stage we could only resolve a personality clash by trooping back into court and asking the judge an irrelevant question, for which we were duly snubbed. In the end, aided by my pointing out that it was Friday afternoon and we would all be locked in for the weekend unless we could agree, only the foreman's patient coaxing saw us through.

However regrettable it may be, I think it fair to record that, after we had delivered our verdict in various cases, as a body of common citizens we were often astonished and sometimes appalled at the leniency of the sentences. This was an interesting reversal of eighteenth- and early nineteenth-century days and, to me, a surprising example of the gap between 'informed opinion' and the rest. Such leniency was sometimes used as an argument for acquittal: 'Why bother to find him guilty if . . .'

Sometimes the verdict did indeed seem irrelevant. We had one tragic sex case where there was no doubt in any of our minds and we duly brought in a reluctant verdict of Guilty. The judge, after considering the previous convictions and the medical evidence, scratched his wig and asked the defence counsel's advice on the sentence. The defence counsel was little help. The wretched defendant was an embarrassment to the law. No one knew what do do with him. Sending him to prison would be futile. Not sending him to prison meant that he would continue flouting the law and be back again in the dock in a few weeks. We were all involved in an insoluble human problem. It was a case, incidentally, of male prostitution and one of those rare occasions when the principal witness proved unable to identify the accused in the box. He wore thick glasses and, try as he might, he simply could not see him. Instead he peered up and down the row of jurymen, causing embarrassment and unease, before slewing off in the direction of the judge who returned his peering with a highly judicial glare.

A charitable word about the police would not come amiss. The danger if the police and judiciary work hand in glove is clear, but there is an opposite extreme. The treatment of police witnesses by counsel several times left me wondering why anyone goes on being a policeman. When the only defence is to convince the jury that the police are a bunch of hardened liars I suppose this is inevitable, but there were occasions when it seemed as though the police were in the dock rather than the accused. One judge ordered a police witness to be reported to his superiors for giving what could be construed as false evidence. This was after a clever counsel had tied him up in verbal knots and even the jury were lost in a maze of double negatives. The bullying of slow-witted men by their intellectual superiors is a nasty aspect of legal practice.

No sooner we were beginning to pride ourselves on becoming professionals than our time was up. This, I presume, is the intention. The juryman is an amateur by definition. On the last day the jury bailiff and his mate unbent and became almost jovial. We were despatched in expectant batches to collect our expenses. Those in the know passed the word round that if a case finished before lunch it was important not to reach a verdict too early. 'Play cards in the jury room for two or three hours,' we were advised. This was to avoid the worst of fates: being empanelled on the last afternoon – a fate which could carry the penalty of serving for several extra days beyond the call of duty.

In retrospect, I think that jurymen must get less consideration than anyone else involved in the courts, the accused not excepted. We were perpetually inconvenienced, kept short of elementary necessities such as a sufficiency of chairs, paper in the lavatories, soap in the basins, and pegs to hang our coats on. Under the threat of dire consequences we were always punctual, yet the courts started late, finished early for lunch, started late again afterwards and finished early at the end of the day; pursuing an unmistakable pattern of maladministration. It seems a pity that lawyers are barred from jury service. If they were not, these matters would soon be put right.

The jury system is one of democracy's safeguards, a protection for all of us against arbitrary conviction by the state. It must be in our own interest that we should sit in judgment on each other. The principle is unexceptionable, and we boast that our legal system, of which it forms a proud part, is the best in the world. One unsung virtue of jury service is that it permits the layman a privileged glimpse of the law's administration and enables him to participate, experiencing at first hand how the whole system actually works. If my ordeal is typical, the practice of the law today leaves a lot to be desired. Reforms are overdue. Unlike lawyers and criminals, jurymen have no axe to grind. They should speak out.

C. H. Rolph

Why me? Had there been any discussion, at some suitable level, of my qualifications as a juror? There had not. No one had considered my age; the Sheriff's Office, who sent out the jury summonses, didn't even know what it was because I had never told them. Nor did they know whether I was a postman, a nun (all these were 'disqualified' from jury service), a doctor, a barrister, a pilot licensed by the Active Elder Brethren of the Corporation of Trinity House of Deptford Strond, a dentist, a midwife, an M.P., or the keeper of a lunatic asylum. In particular they didn't know whether I was a person who was or had been in the police service, which I was. The small blue document required me 'to be of a jury to try between our Sovereign Lady the Queen and the Several Defendants and Prisoners to be at the Bar', at what was then known as the Quarter Sessions of the Peace for the County of London and was very soon to be rechristened the Inner London Crown Court. 'Whereof fail not,' tartly concluded the small blue document, 'as you will answer the contrary at your peril.'

I would not fail them. The British are divided into two main groups, those longing to serve on a jury and those who will stoop to any trick to get out of it. Some fault in the system keeps them eternally separate and apart. The longing ones are never called and the unwilling ones spend their lives trying in vain to escape. At the time I belonged to the first group; partly because for many years I had studied jurors at the Old Bailey without ever discovering what they really did, and partly because I was now a journalist and always in need of a subject.

On the appointed morning at nine-fifteen, therefore, I stood with upwards of two hundred others in a court room built to accommodate forty men and a boy, waiting in the intense

English silence of non-acquaintanceship for we knew not what. Heavy footsteps at last heralded the arrival of a large, friendly man in wig and gown whom at first I did not recognize though I had known him for years. He was Leo Burgess, formerly an official in the Public Office at the Old Bailey, and now Clerk of the Peace for the County of London. (Since 1972 this official has been called, much less picturesquely, the Court Administrator. This is a betrayal of legal history, but luckily Mr Burgess has retired, with the warm good wishes of everyone who knows him.) He said good morning and told us something of the duties that lay before us, and we listened intently. Then we were marshalled into dozens, so that each dozen could be given a date on which to come back and start work. After which I met Mr Burgess in a long corridor.

'What are *you* doing here?' he said, though the words sounded much more affable than they look. I told him I was one of the jurors for the session. 'Oh no, you're not,' he said. 'You're a cop, and that disqualifies you.' No longer, I announced: I was out of the police, and writing for a living. He insisted that this made no difference. Once a cop, always a cop. The considerations that made it undesirable to have policemen on juries didn't suddenly go away the moment a man ceased to be a policeman. I knew that this was too logical to have been enshrined in the law. I insisted, with a confidence made easier by the fact that he was a man with absolutely no self-importance and a delightful sense of humour, that I was entitled to serve and should, if turned away, make a terrible fuss in the *New Statesman.* He had no time just then to discuss the Juries Act with me, but said if it turned out that I *was* disqualified he would see that I was notified in good time to save me a futile second journey to the court. I received no notification; perhaps because Mr Burgess found that, as an ex-cop, or even as a serving cop, I was not disqualified – I was merely 'exempted'. All this has now changed. I should be 'ineligible' today; ineligible since April 1st, 1974, when the relevant parts of the Criminal Justice Act 1972 were brought into operation. And if I now proceeded to serve on a jury in a criminal court, knowing I was ineligible, I could be fined £100. So could High Court judges; barristers and solicitors, practising or not; court shorthand-writers; clergymen and nuns; and a long list of people who might be supposed to know anything whatever about the law – the supreme disqualification for jury service being some knowledge of the law that juries must help to administer.

'You were lucky,' said the jury bailiff on my next appearance. 'If we don't want someone serving on juries here,' he added darkly, 'we've got ways of seeing that he doesn't.' One of them, no doubt, was simply to leave him sitting in the jurors' waiting room every day for the fortnight to three weeks of the session, never once putting his name in the box.

My jury, with whom I was to serve for three weeks and try about fifteen cases, included three women: one of them sharp, thin, cynical, suspicious of the whole world and very annoyed at being there at all; the other two comfortable, motherly, ingenuous and bewildered about everything except the need that, from our second day onwards, we should all have cups of tea when we retired to consider our verdicts. Since these were neither supplied nor available, they took it in turns to bring, in a big shopping bag which also contained knitting, a huge Thermos jug of hot tea, a pint of milk, a cocoa-tin full of sugar, and some mugs and spoons. By the fourth day we men were coming with buns and biscuits to fill out the occasion. I don't know how typical this is, but it may come as a revelation to the Lord Chancellor, the judges, the 'court administrators', and all those others who insist that the efficacy of the jury system depends entirely on the secrecy of what they get up to in their room.

I told no one of my police experience. I was a journalist. But I was in a strange and (I thought) interesting situation, which the law was soon to make no longer possible. I was determined to enjoy it, finding out everything I possibly could about the jury system as an institution whose survival, it already seemed to me, challenged commonsense and logic at every point. But although I told no one of my past, I was among twelve people who were very puzzled and slightly apprehensive about their duties, and who were all asking each other questions. When they asked me a question whose answer I had known for years, I sometimes found myself replying with the confidence of an 'old sweat'; and, putting this down to some supposed experience as a court reporter (for they knew I was a journalist), they began looking to me as some kind of make-do oracle.

They should have needed no oracle. They should have had a booklet or pamphlet telling them why they were there, how they had been chosen, what they couldn't do, why they would have to sit silent and useless when a prisoner pleaded guilty (and therefore needed no jury), why they would have nothing to do with the sentences that would be passed on prisoners, what expenses and allowances they could claim, what to do if they found themselves unable to agree on a verdict, and how to keep awake after a pub lunch when listening to a two-hour speech about fraudulent conversion. So far as I know, they still get no such booklet. What they may get, at a court administered by someone as conscientious as Mr Leo Burgess, is a ten-minute 'headmaster's chat' on the first morning of term, of which the only item to secure lodgment in their minds will be the bit about allowances and expenses.

Until 1933 there was an institution called the Grand Jury, which was then abolished (to the grief of the traditionalists) as a useless and timewasting historical curiosity. The Grand Jury, perhaps because it was so grand (it comprised twenty-three local bigwigs and landowners), got a great deal more instruction than the trial juries ever did, or ever will. It was a 'jury of presentment', its ancestor was the baronial 'hundred' whose tithing-men at one time caught the prisoners and brought them to trial; and all it had to decide was whether, in the case of every prisoner for trial, the Crown had made out a reasonable case to answer. It got through all its work in a day, sometimes in a morning, hearing only the prosecution's side – and usually, at that, only a brief statement from one police officer – saying 'True Bill' when it was satisfied about a case and 'No Bill' when it was not. And yet it would be given, on the opening morning of the session, a long harangue from the Bench which was known as 'charging the Grand Jury' and which – give or take an hour or so in which the judge declared his views on the current state of crime, education, public morality, and perhaps low-cut blouses – was devoted to a description of their duties and what was expected of them, which wasn't much . . . No trial jury (or 'petty jury' as it was rather slightingly called) has ever had such careful instruction before or since the abolition of the Grand Jury; but it is the trial jury that needs it. I would suggest that if, for some reason, jurors can't be given a booklet of instructions (which they could be required to hand back at the end of the session, if it's expense that we are worried about), then they should be given, during a full day preceding the opening of the session, a long question-and-answer seminar on their forthcoming duties. As it is, they approach those duties in a state of some bewilderment, learning the job at the expense of luckless prisoners or still more luckless prosecutors. Trial and error can't possibly be the best way to teach them, if their role is as vital as their apologists maintain.

The jury bailiff took us into a little room and told us to choose our foreman. While we were wondering how you did this, he said to the best-dressed man among us, 'Would *you* like to be foreman, sir?' And the best-dressed man made a deprecating noise. We all said yes, he would be the best foreman, and then the bailiff told us a few things we *must not* do. One of these was get up in court and ask questions (the judges didn't like that): if there was something we wanted to ask, we must write it on a piece of paper and have an usher pass it to the judge. What piece of paper? Was it supplied or did one use the back of an envelope? Ah well, a piece could probably be found, but most jurors seemed to tear a leaf out of a diary, or something. The main thing was that there must be no standing up and talking. Little jurors were to be seen and not heard.

That was all, then: ten o'clock tomorrow, ladies and gentlemen. And then one of our number spoke up. All this was going to ruin him, he said. He ran a one-man business, and no one could stand in for him. We all stopped chatting while he developed the theme, in rising tones of desperation. But why hadn't he said so before, asked the jury bailiff? We had all been told we could ask for exemption or postponement – did he not hear? Yes, but there had seemed to be hundreds of people around and he was shy. The bailiff took him away to have the hardship investigated ('that's what I'm here for'), and we never saw him again. Another man told me in a whisper that he himself was over age – he was seventy-six – but rather welcomed the experience as an alternative to sitting in the local recreation ground or public library while the married daughter who tended his widowerhood did the housework at home. Did I think he would get into trouble if his age were discovered? I thought not; and even today, the Criminal Justice Act of 1972 says no more than that he must tell the truth if they *ask* how old he is. Failing that, only the use of an ear-trumpet would have been likely to betray him.

I heard later that a member of another jury (not mine) at the same session had been sacked from his job when he told his employer, an orthopaedic surgeon with a small practice, that he was to be absent for two or three weeks on jury service. By some discreet process the court officers saw to it that he was reinstated in his job, and it may be that the employer's attention was directed to the remarks of Mr Justice Melford Stevenson in a similar case at Sussex Assizes in July 1966. The employer had been brought before his lordship on a charge of contempt of court:

> If I had thought you seriously threatened to sack an employee if he obeyed a jury summons, nothing would have saved you from going to prison for a substantial period. You have expressed sincere regret . . . I propose to accept the apology and say no more about it. Any future conduct of this kind will be followed by very grave consequences. What you did is, among other things, a deplorable exhibition of ignorance on the part of a responsible person. *The Times,* July 29th, 1966.

But it would be slightly more difficult, some of us reflected, to prevent an unreasonable, angry and stupid employer from sacking the man later; or from filling his job with a 'temporary', finding he had thus acquired a better man, and deciding that there wasn't room for both of them.

And then, when it was time to go home at the end of that first day, we all discovered that we went the same way and were in fact near neighbours. We all, in the local register of electors, had the letter 'J' against our names because we paid rates and hadn't claimed any exemptions. Now that all voters over eighteen are liable, there won't be any more 'Js' in the voting lists and the range of choice will be enormous. But it still won't be haphazard: the oft-proclaimed principle of 'random selection' which is held to be vital to the system and has always been conspicuously absent from it will, to coin a phrase, be more absent than ever. Before April 1st, 1974, the summoning authorities – the County Sheriff or a firm of solicitors to whom they might delegate the job – used a variety of systems of their own invention and as complicated as a pools permutation. One would summon, for this month, all the householders living at odd numbers in Crescents, Avenues or Gardens. Next month the evens. The month after that, the odds from Roads and Terraces. And so it went on. Another office, picking out twenty adjacent roads, would take all the As from the first, the Bs from the second, and work through the alphabet until there were enough. Another office just used a pin. Ours must have worked on the adjacent-roads principle and we all came from Blackheath, London.

It was done differently for the Old Bailey, which has most of the Home Counties area to choose from. When an Old Bailey jury decided in 1968 that *Last Exit to Brooklyn* was an obscene book unredeemed by any literary merit, Mr John Calder, who had published it, complained that the jury was drawn entirely from the East End of London and was thus 'incompetent to judge a serious work of literature'. He may have based this assessment on the dialect accent in which they severally took the juror's oath: but this is a treacherous guide today, for what used to be called a Cockney accent can now be heard from Dover to Oxford and Portsmouth to Harwich. And he provoked the clerk of the court at the Old Bailey, Mr Leslie Boyd, to write to *The Times* and put the record straight. The *Last Exit* jury was in fact drawn, said Mr Boyd, from East Ham, Plaistow, Stoke Newington, Sidcup, Chislehurst, Uxbridge, Harrow and Kingston-upon-Thames. And this information, he added, had been supplied to Mr Calder's counsel at the trial, in accordance with usual practice.

We began trying cases. For the first day my colleagues were all attention; interested, anxious, rather sceptical and, above all, worried about the inaudibility of witnesses. There was one nervous lady, a witness for the Crown in a case of 'employment fraud', whom none of us could hear. 'You *will* speak up, won't you?' she was constantly asked by prosecuting counsel. 'It's essential, you see, that my lord and the jury should hear what you are saying.' I thought it was a bit more essential for us than for his lordship, who, after all, had seen the depositions (the evidence taken earlier by the magistrates); it was all totally new to us. 'Yes,' she said timidly each time, and went on with her answers in precisely the same way. When we were at lunch in a neighbouring pub, rashly ingesting soporific quantities of steak-and-kidney pudding, our foreman asked me if I could hear the poor woman's evidence. I couldn't hear it at all, I said. 'Neither can I,' he admitted; 'so what the hell's the use of that?

What do we do? Pass a note to the judge saying we've heard nothing she has said? She's been giving evidence for more than an hour.' We decided that it was the only thing to do, and on our return he gave the court usher a note accordingly.

'Oh dear,' said the judge. 'Are you saying you've heard nothing this witness has said?'

'Very little, my lord,' said the foreman, and we all shook our heads meaning yes, neither had we. The judge said he wished we had told him before; and the foreman, greatly daring, made two observations that seemed to us unanswerable. First, we had all been very much discouraged about interrupting the proceedings or addressing the judge, even on bits of paper. Second, we had hoped when the witness began that she would improve as she gained confidence. The judge said nothing about the bits of paper, but he and the court officials went into a huddle. Then he asked both counsel whether they would agree that the shorthand-writer should read back the whole of the poor lady's evidence, and they did. (This always seems to me, by the way, as a shorthand-writer of sorts myself, a prodigious feat that the shorthand-writers can nevertheless always perform with effortless and almost insulting ease.) And once the reading-back had brought us to the point reached by the lunch adjournment, both counsel thenceforward repeated loudly every answer that the witness – and indeed subsequent witnesses – gave.

I remember, by the way, being told by a juror, after the conviction of Lord Kylsant at the Old Bailey in 1936 on a charge of publishing a false company prospectus, that he had not heard one syllable of Mr Justice Wright's *sotto voce,* six-hour summing-up. And having been present in court at various times while that summing-up was going on, I remember being astonished that the learned judge could hear it himself.

On the third morning one of our colleagues was twenty minutes late and a part-heard trial was in progress without him. Our hearts were with him as he crept, scarlet-faced, to his seat and sank into it. We supposed that either the prosecution or the defence could have objected to going on with eleven jurors, but since they had not objected, his presence among us when he did turn up was superfluous and he might as well have made a day of it and gone to Lord's. But no one said a word to him, the blush gradually went from his cheeks, and by way of rehabilitating himself he listened to the rest of the proceedings with an ostentatious intensity which, sad to say, was totally wasted. 'I'm afraid you don't really count any more, on this case,' our foreman cheerfully told him when we retired to consider our verdict and have our mugs of home-made coffee. 'They decided to go on without you, and so you haven't heard all the evidence.' His train was late, he said miserably. But the rest of us, all (like him) from Blackheath station, had been on an earlier train, which wasn't late. He was in an H.M. Bateman situation, and was lucky not to be serving under an H.M. Bateman judge. He seemed a broken man after that, a man apart.

Two trials later I myself was faced with a poser. The prisoner, charged with a Post Office Savings Bank fraud, was a man I knew. This, by itself, would probably be enough to justify, indeed to require, a bit of paper from myself to the judge saying that the prisoner was personally known to me and that perhaps I should leave the jury? But I might be asked to state the capacity or the connection in which I knew him. (You don't get off a jury quite so easily as that, or not every time.) This would have involved saying that I had seen him acquitted on a similar charge, years before, at the Old Bailey. Totally unfair to the prisoner, who might never have made any other court appearance. It would be unfair enough if the Old Bailey appearance had ended in a conviction, but an acquittal must *never* be mentioned at any stage, by anyone; its prejudicial impact is hardly less than that of a previous conviction and yet the man might be completely innocent, on the present charge no less than on the earlier one. Nor was that all. If the judge wanted to know how and where I knew the man, it might come out that I was a former police officer; and there would be an argument as to whether I should leave the jury box in some ignominy instead of leaving it as a public-spirited citizen anxious to uphold the law in all its pristine purity. I *think* the judge would have been bound to find (as the law was then) that I was not disqualified; but I dithered too long, the trial was getting under way, and I let it go. In the event, and much to my relief, the jury were unanimous in acquitting the man.

Unanimous? There were three men on our jury who wanted to acquit everybody and were slightly unhappy, obviously, each time they gave way. They distrusted the police, were overborne by the eloquence of defending counsel, and fastened eagerly on the judge's very proper but routine references to the 'benefit of the doubt' and proof 'beyond reasonable doubt'. They seemed to feel that, human nature being as it is, there could never be a case that was free from doubt. There had been a run of cases (there have been some more lately) in which juries had convicted and then, sometimes months or even years later, another man already in prison had confessed to the crime – and, which is always important, his confession had been checked by the police and verified in every tiny detail. I believe that, before the law of England was changed (in 1967) to allow 'majority verdicts' as in Scotland, there were in effect thousands of majority verdicts reflecting the uneasy complicity of timid or bewildered jurors whose doubts might have been well-founded. The truth is that once you admit the principle of majority verdicts you are admitting the responsibility of convicting people *in spite of reasonable doubt.* This at least was done in 1967 by legislators with their eyes wide open, for the point was canvassed often enough during the debates on Section 13 of the Criminal Justice Act. The reasonable doubts of two jury members – and it might be the absolute certainty, as they saw it, of two jury members – were quietly written off.

At the same time it's the experience of everyone who has served on a criminal jury that it gets tougher as it gains experience. Towards the end of every session at any Crown Court (I am credibly told) and at the Old Bailey (I can say from experience), the proportion of convictions goes up. And towards the end of my short period of jury service at the County of London Sessions, defending counsel were getting fed up with us.

You hear little (since jurors talk so little) about the hideous embarrassment of listening for hours to the formal and platitudinous rhetoric of young men in snow-white wigs. (The wigs get darker as their owners move on to more important and better-paid work.) But my fellow-jurors seemed to find this especially hard to take. 'You really don't know where to look, do you?' said my foreman towards the end of the session. 'You've heard it all before, you can't believe a lot of it, and generally you know the chap's wasting his time – and yours.' I remember that when we said 'Guilty' at the end of one case, defending counsel (in an off-white wig) flung his pencil down with a clatter and was looked at sternly by the judge. It seemed sometimes to matter more to the barrister than to the prisoner that there should be a triumphant and wildly improbable acquittal. For my part, I found it possible to feel very sorry for some of the younger barristers, left by their elder 'brothers-in-law' to make bricks without straw; but it was a feeling which merely sharpened the embarrassment.

Equally embarrassing was the conduct – innocent enough though it may be – of police witnesses who, having given evidence, were required to remain in court for fear that they might confer with others who had not. 'In court' is the last place they should be, unless they can be kept strictly out of the jury's vision. Several times they sat in a row exactly opposite the jury box, and when the prisoner or his supporting witnesses were giving evidence the silent laughter and rolling eyes of these knowing policemen, and their other gestures of derisive disbelief, were such as to make some jurymen, at any rate, feel that they were being taken for a ride by the whole court process. There is absolutely no doubt in my mind that witnesses, police or other, who have given evidence should be kept out of the jury's sight until the case is over. The deadpan facial control of court clerks and ushers is something acquired by practice: and if they failed to acquire it they would not be clerks or ushers for very long.

But the greatest enemy of justice in the courts is drowsiness; or, not to put too fine a point upon it, downright slumber. In the afternoon it is sometimes impossible to keep awake, not merely in the jury box but on the judicial bench – many times I have seen judges and magistrates fast asleep during a trial, and more than once there have been appeals to the Court of Appeal on the ground that the trial judge was asleep. (I don't remember that any of these has succeeded.) Sometimes the sleepers manage to perfect a private technique in concealing their condition; one well-known woman magistrate in London could not merely sleep sitting bolt upright but *always* woke up at precisely three-fifteen to make some loud observation she hoped was relevant (which it surprisingly often was). Once when she did this in a Juvenile Court she woke up at a moment when a young detective constable was in the witness box. She looked at him over her spectacles. 'You look a *very* big boy for fourteen?' she said.

Lord Justice Birkett told me in a radio inverview that

drowsiness in the criminal courts was the second greatest cause of injustice. The first was crime itself. Speaking 'off the air' on the same occasion, he gave me a frightening story which now falls, I suppose, into the 'now-it-can-be-told' class. During the war he was chairman of the Home Office Committee which heard and decided appeals against orders for internment on the Isle of Man under Defence Regulation 18B. During one such hearing the appellant, a Czechoslovakian tailor who was thought to be 'of hostile origin and association' (though as to this Lord Birkett had grave misgivings), produced a long typewritten document and said he wanted to read it to the Tribunal and that it would take about an hour. Lord Birkett glanced at the clock. It was lunchtime. 'Very well,' he said, 'but perhaps you had better make a start on that after lunch.'

After the resumption, the man had been reading in his halting, monotonous broken English for about half an hour when he suddenly stopped. 'Well?' said the chairman. 'Go on. You are doing very well.' The man gestured towards the other members of the Tribunal. 'With you perhaps, Mr Chairman,' he said, 'but just look at your colleagues.' Lord Birkett looked round at them, and they were all slumped in their chairs, fast asleep. 'I took the papers from him,' he said, 'and we all read out a page each until it was finished. And thus only did we keep awake. The man was literally on trial for his freedom. It was simply awful.'

And awful it is: a mockery of 'justice' for which, it seems generally to be thought, there can be no cure and which is accepted by 'the system' with the resignation we can always rely upon in enduring the misfortunes of others. But because I think that resignation is not the answer, and that a sleeping court is neither excusable nor funny, I offer a cure for sleepy jurors on the assumption that they at least will be with us for very many years to come. They should never be allowed alcohol at lunch; they should be given small and non-soporific meals on the court premises; at the discretion of the judge they should change seats with each other every fifteen minutes during a trial; and they should be not merely allowed, but *required*, to take notes of the evidence. The notes might not be any good in themselves, but the making of them would be a refuge from boredom, embarrassment, the feeling of helplessness and the curse of drowsiness.

William Solesbury

It was the extraordinary ordinariness of everybody called for jury service that first impressed me. It was a feeling that lasted the whole fortnight, although obviously in time one got to know certain individuals rather better, to note characteristics other than their appearance or surface manner as the main indication of what they were like. In time, also, people sorted themselves into groups, and towards the end of the second week, when all two hundred or so jurors were gathered together before being allocated to juries for the day, the *Telegraph* readers or housewives or young men or old men noticeably formed little clusters.

But on the first morning I arrived in the central hall of the court building to find myself amongst an apparently complete sample of the population. Whatever the process of selecting jurors, it must be fairly random. Here was the result. A group of people all different in size, age, colour, states of health, degrees of cleverness, levels of wealth, styles of dress, manners of speech, personal habits, tastes, interests, experiences, careers and anything and everything else. The only thing they had in common was being in that place at that time for that purpose.

And this, I realized after a while, was why the sensation of being among such a seemingly unselective cross section of the community was so odd. For almost everywhere else I go – my workplace, the trains and buses I ride, the shops I use, the doctor's waiting room, the cinemas, the homes of friends – the other people have for the most part something, and usually a lot, in common with me. This is just because like people tend to do like things in like places. They do so out of choice. But one doesn't do jury service out of choice. It is one of the few obligations in life that is hard to evade. And so there was this strange and rare phenomenon that so intrigued me – the jury as the great leveller! As things turned out it was an impression that underlay many subsequent feelings about the experience of jury service.

The randomness is maintained by the jury bailiff's twice-daily reallocations of waiting jurors to juries. It seems to be a popular impression that the same jury serves on a succession of trials. In fact the jury bailiff reshuffles the juries all the time. He does this literally, by having all the jurors' names on playing-card size buff cards. As with all but the most expert card shufflers, some cards stick together and you can find yourself in familiar company through a succession of shuffles. But sooner or later you get parted from those whom you have made companions. The process is further complicated by the frequency with which courts have no need of juries allocated to them, and by the process of selecting twelve jurors from the eighteen possibles allocated to a court.

It becomes an obstacle race actually to get on a jury. And after a day or more of sitting around one gets very anxious to succeed. It goes like this. To start with, at the beginning of the morning or the afternoon, all those jurors not on a serving jury engaged on a continuing case will be allocated by the jury bailiff to a waiting jury, eighteen strong. Most of these are then ordered to a particular court. Some are told to hang around as spare juries. Spare juries were rarely called and this effectively meant you'd failed to clear the first obstacle and must simply wait until dismissed to return after lunch or next morning to try again. The waiting juries go and wait at a court until they are needed. If you're lucky you wait inside a court and so have the court proceedings to interest you; if not, you wait outside or in the jury room. But the court may not need a jury that morning or afternoon – previous cases go on longer than estimated, defendants plead guilty, the 'business' is something other than trials. In that case you've failed at the second obstacle. But you may get called into a court which needs a jury. The clerk of the court then shuffles the eighteen name cards and orders twelve into the jury box. The remaining six have failed at the third obstacle – though there is a slight chance that one of the twelve may be objected to. If that happens then you've failed at the fourth and last obstacle and one of the rejected six is called to take your place. If you clear the fourth obstacle, then you're away and can only hope for an interesting case.

Racing is perhaps the wrong metaphor to use for a process with so much waiting around. The time spent waiting is exhausting and, where I was, you waited in inadequate and uncomfortable surroundings. Spare juries waited in the canteen. At least the seats were canvas there. Outside the courts there were frequently only wooden benches. Inside the courts the seats were more comfortable.

It is curious how familiar court-room proceedings seem – I suppose after seeing so many T.V. and film court-room dramas. The traditional and awesome majesty of the law must have been quite devalued in this way. And the awkward formality of the typical court-room arrangement, everything at right angles, with successive benches towering above each other with the judge himself on the loftiest pinnacle of all, designed presumably to overawe all the participants, seems no odder or less familiar than the London Palladium or Lord's Cricket Ground. Really this must be a good thing, especially for the jury who have to approach their act of judgment with impartiality. All that traditional stage management is designed to elevate the law with the judge literally on a throne, to provide a platform for those testifying in public in the witness stand, either as plaintiffs or defendants, and to denigrate the defendant, caged in his box and flanked by policemen. Newer court rooms are less extreme in their architectural symbolism but the same elements are there, even if the judge is set only two feet – not twelve feet – above the floor of the court room and the defendant's box is not railed.

Because all this has been reduced to a staple component of T.V. soap operas, it can more easily be taken in the juror's stride. At the time of my service, a series of *Justice* with Margaret Lockwood had just finished on T.V. and this provided the essential frame of reference for most jurors. Lady barristers were invaribly greeted with whispers of 'Here comes Margaret Lockwood' while the flashier young male barristers were compared to Anthony Valentine. All this is doubtless a matter of much regret to lawyers, but to my mind it humanizes the whole business. For the jurors much turns on their general attitudes towards the participants in court proceedings – towards judges, barristers, defendants, the police and witnesses. Some of these attitudes were surprising – in particular the widespread distrust of the police and the degree of sympathy for defendants.

Most jurors seemed to have a half-amused view of judges. Certainly of all those involved judges are the most stereotyped and caricatured. People seem to expect them to be aged, remote, deaf and vicious. Consequently it is when they turn out to have other characteristics than these – if they look friendly or sound lucid – that it is a matter for comment. This is undoubtedly unfair. But it is nevertheless the terrible performances by judges which stick in the mind. In particular, a really bad summing-up does a great disservice to the cause of justice. For example, what seemed relatively simple legal issues in the case of a warehouse employee who had conspired in the theft of goods from the warehouse were totally mangled in the judge's summing-up. There was no structure to his presentation, no attempt to pinpoint the key points of law. Great chunks of fat law books were read out without any attempt being made to translate or interpret them; extraordinary diversions, including a long lament for the passing of the Clapham omnibus and the man on it, were delivered, and total irrelevancies such as a fulsome expression of sympathy for some witness who had not been able to travel up from Torquay on account of fibrositis were included. The jurors were not only confused, but bored, and the judge's essential contribution to the trial through his summing-up was missing. To be fair, a woman judge in a quite complex case gave a masterly summing-up, exposing the points at issue with a thoroughness and logic which provided a frame for the jurors' consideration of the case, without which they might well have decided badly and unfairly.

All judges seem to come on strong when it comes to sentencing. Even the light sentences are handed down with calls for gratitude for the leniency received or fierce threats of far worse next time. It is with sentencing that judges are most closely associated and their actions in this respect tend to determine their general reputations, ranked on a scale from lenient to harsh. But, for the jury, the judge's role in interpreting the law and distilling the essence of the prosecution and defence cases is far more important.

Jurors' attitudes towards barristers seem much more straightforward. Basically, they are regarded as being there to do a job. The fact that both prosecution and defence counsel sit together on the same bench, dress alike, chat to each other in a friendly manner and generally behave cooperatively reinforces the feeling that they are paid advocates for one cause or another but with no personal commitment. In that sense they appear to the jury in a very different light from the judge or the defendant – the judge being committed to maintaining justice, the defendant to saving his skin. These are the protagonists with something to gain or lose; the barristers are just hired guns.

Examples of professional incompetence help to reinforce this impression of a lack of commitment. In one case no counsel for the defence had appeared when the case was due to be heard. The judge was incensed and insisted that inquiries were made of the defendant's solicitors. The message came back that the partner in charge had gone on holiday but a junior of the firm was on his way to court. He turned out to be a youth of nineteen or so, obviously appalled at what 'keeping an eye on the office for the morning' had turned out to involve. He got a fierce lecture from the judge and the case was put back until the solicitor returned from his holiday and got round to appointing a counsel for his client. Another incident was scarcely more reassuring. On this occasion there was again great delay in starting the case and the jury were kept waiting in the corridor outside the court room, mingling with the police and the witnesses. Suddenly a barrister arrived in a great flurry, accompanied by a junior from the solicitors, to be rushed into the room where it was apparent the defendant was locked. After a while they emerged and with scarcely lowered voices discussed, in front of the waiting jurors, police and witnesses, what defence to offer. After a few minutes, back they went into the room, then out again, more discussion and consultation of law books. After a few repeats of this sequence of events, the trial started. Quite clearly this was, for some reason or another, the first meeting between defendant and counsel. Not surprisingly the defence was not well done and, having witnessed the whole business, every member of the jury knew why.

The impression created by barristers is that they do their job without overmuch enthusiasm. I suppose that the bread-and-butter business of a big city Crown Court – mostly assaults, break-ins, cheque forging, receiving and such like – is not the most exciting or demanding challenge for barristers. Yet all the forms of legal dispute are there, particularly the right to cross-examine. Somehow, however, it never seems to come to life. Even the occasional heightened language – 'Come now, is it not so that what you have told us here is nothing more than a fabrication, a veritable pack of lies?' – is delivered in a tired and not very convincing manner. It is hard after a fortnight of listening to these usually competent but almost always dull presentations of their clients' cases to believe in the persuasive power of advocacy. In that respect the court-room drama does not live up to its T.V. and film versions.

In this situation, the defendant is very much left to make his own impression on the jury. The fundamental principle of criminal justice is 'innocent till proved guilty'. Everybody knows this and there can hardly be a juror who does not remind himself and his fellow jurors of it from time to time. But this principle is given real force when allied to that other maxim, 'There but for the grace of God go I.' It only needs knowledge of a few cases to convince one how easily one can find oneself on the wrong side of the law.

There was the case of the man, undoubtedly drunk, who remonstrated with the police about the arrest of his even drunker friend, only to find himself loaded into the van as well and later in a fight with the duty officers at the station. The charge was assault on a policeman and it was dismissed on the jury's suspicion that it was the defendant who had been assaulted by the police. There was another man up on two charges: a principal charge of receiving stolen carpets and a second of having pencils and inks belonging to his employer in his room. The first charge was dropped and the jury never learned why, but the second, which arose out of the police search of his room on suspicion about the carpets, was pressed. And who has not in their home a few items of one kind or another taken from their workplace? There was a young man employed at a warehouse who, when left in charge by his boss for a day or two, was foolish enough to boast of his responsibility in a pub; whereupon he became the unwilling accessory before the fact to a pair of thugs intent on stealing the contents.

There were others more immediately and obviously culpable. But there was enough uncertainty about the facts, enough evidence of malevolent chance to reinforce the natural sympathy of a jury for the defendant. Many jurors in conversation inside and outside the jury rooms would allude to knowledge of experiences with the police similar to that of the defendant. The formula was, 'There's a young bloke in our flats who . . .' or 'My brother-in-law was caught that way . . .' or 'There was a case in our local paper . . .' but one frequently suspected that the experience put at some distance in these ways was really closer to home. Most people, I suppose, have had some fairly close experience with the law, usually arising out of motoring offences. Consequently it is with the defendant that the juror has most sympathy and can most closely identify. In only one case was the opposite view observable. A juror taking a very hard line against a van driver charged with damaging a parked vehicle revealed, in the course of a long dispute with his fellow jurors, that he had once been found guilty on a similar charge and he was damned if this chap was going to get away with it.

The jury's identification with the defendant combines with the cross-sectional character of the jurors to force one to the conclusion that there are no such things as the criminal classes. Outside a court room the jurors and witnesses, and even the defendant, if he is not in custody, can mingle and are indistinguishable from each other. It is the barristers, the judges and the police in their uniforms who are so evidently different. They are the professionals in the whole business. The jurors, witnesses and defendants are alike in their amateur status, making a once-only appearance. Inside the court, when their separate roles have been more clearly defined, an ignorant observer might easily conclude on visual evidence alone that the defendant had been picked from the jury. In comparison with all the others in their fancy dress he has most in common with the jurors. As with the interior architecture of the court room, the appearance of things has a symbolic importance.

Part of this feeling for the defendant is related to a distrust of the police. Few jurors seem prepared to believe that, in principle, the police are truthful. Others had warned me of a tendency among jurors to accept the fact of prosecution as evidence of guilt – the 'no smoke without fire' argument. My experience was quite contrary to this. Sometimes from personal experience, sometimes from mild anarchism, or sometimes from a radical commitment to individual rights, the police side of any story was frequently viewed by jurors with a suspicion which the presumption of innocence alone could not justify.

A number of aspects of court procedure reinforce this gut reaction. The invariable reliance of police witnesses on their notes, with routine assurance that they had been made within hours of the events, can so easily seem to imply calculated collusion and fabrication. In contrast, defendant and witnesses have never had the presence of mind to prepare notes. The frequency with which charges are dropped at the start of proceedings, presumably because an insufficient case has been put together since the charges were made, undermines the general faith in the police. Likewise, the addition of secondary charges, such as breaking some glasses as well as grievously harming a man in a pub brawl, or being in possession of stolen pencils as well as carpets, gives an impression that the police are intent on making something stick. This is undoubtedly unfair since these actions both arise from the necessity to bring charges quickly after an arrest is made and before all the evidence is in. Nevertheless, it still leaves the juror with a distrustful attitude towards the police.

This cynicism about the police is reinforced by the feeling that they alone have no right to give biased accounts, suppress facts, speak falsehoods. Jurors seem to expect little devotion to the truth from counsel. They are there to do their hirer's bidding. The defendant himself is of course going to lie to some degree: what else should he do if his skin is at risk? But the police have no such excuses which the juror can accept, for their excuses are all external to the trial in hand: keeping up the statistics on convictions, getting known habitual criminals put away on some charge or other, covering up rough treatment, loyalty to colleagues and so on.

These attitudes towards the participants are important elements in the jurors' decision-making. Their general feelings about judges, barristers, police and defendant, both as they were held before jury service and as they develop during it, must be brought to bear on the facts of the particular case and the demeanour and actions in court of the particular participants. Judges remind juries time and again of the nature of their duties: to satisfy themselves on the facts of the case and beyond reasonable doubt of the guilt or innocence of the defendant as charged. None of the elements in this statement of duty are clear cut: in particular the facts are rarely certain and the legal issues relating to the charge seldom crystal clear.

Criminal trials demonstrate again and again what an uncertain quantity the so-called facts are. In cases where two opposing parties – the police and the defendant – are the sole witnesses one would expect dispute about the facts, whether honest or dishonest. But apart from this it is extraordinary how lacking in corroboration, how open to different honest interpretation, how partial and fragmentary the facts surrounding offences can be. The jury has no right of cross-examination so that its doubts about the facts as presented remain unanswered, unless it adopts the course of returning to the court from the jury room to seek further guidance from the judge. That will often not seem justified. Nevertheless the missing pieces in the evidence add to their unease at reaching a decision. In one case, nobody explained what had occurred during the fifteen minutes which elapsed after the police followed suspected smash-and-grab raiders into a jeweller's in trading hours and before they seized them: they can hardly have just stood staring at each other. In another case a woman was called as a witness to a pub fight. Before she was called she was billed by the prosecution as the defendant's girlfriend, but when she was cross-examined she was treated as an uninvolved bystander. Hardly a case arises in which some part of the story, sometimes crucial, sometimes not, clearly remains untold.

The legal issues can be equally obscure. Much here depends on the judge's summing-up. The defence in the pub brawl case was temporary insanity through drunkenness – on the face of it an absurdity. Yet the legal technicalities surrounding this quite admissible defence were in fact extremely tricky. About six different tests were identified by the judge which the defence would need to pass for it to succeed. Even the simple everyday charges – like breaking and entering, assault and battery, and receiving – can involve legal niceties on which innocence or guilt can turn. Often it is not simply a matter for the jury to decide if the defendant was there and committed some act, but about deciding if what he did was, in legal terms, criminal or not – usually a far stiffer nut to crack. The juror soon learns that guilt and innocence have meanings beyond their everyday usage.

Two further things add to the prevailing uncertainty: the jury is ignorant of the defendant's background and has no influence over the sentence. The jury never learns anything about the defendant other than his name and the details of the alleged crime until after the verdict is given. Then, as a preliminary to the judge's sentence, the prosecution recites any list of previous convictions and the defence tells the tale of his life – parentage, upbringing, education, jobs, marriages, homes and so on. This is an important moment for the jury, for these revelations can confirm their judgment based on the demeanour of the defendant in court and the facts of the case alone. When a list of previous convictions as long as your arm is read out against the defendant, they realize that they'd suspected all along he was a bad sort; when the terrible facts of childhood abandonment, uncompleted education, successive unemployment and failed human relationships are paraded, they know they were right in thinking him a sad case. It is a moment of real emotional release for the jury after the strain of reaching a verdict and passing judgment with potentially severe consequences on a fellow human being.

The verdict and the sentence are kept separate in court procedure. For the jury there is only the one choice between guilt and innocence. In reality, the frequent uncertainty of the facts, the legal niceties and sense of identity between jurors and defendant, constantly bring home to them the realization that the distinction is too simple-minded. Rather, there is a range from total innocence to direct guilt. Most defendants come somewhere in the middle, are fairly innocent or pretty guilty. So the juror thinks that he'd have none of those reasonable doubts if he could only be confident that the sentence would not be too heavy. In part this is undoubtedly an attempt to ease some of the burden of deciding the defendant's fate, a desire to minimize the harm done should a mistake be made. But it also represents an honest expression of the juror's reaction to being forced to think and decide solely in terms of two extreme conditions, without the intermediate states. So the judge's sentencing, as much as the revelation of the personal history of the defendant, provides a very charged moment for the jury. Only then do they learn what punishment their decision has brought on the defendant.

In many ways the worst part of being a juror is not in the jury room arguing it out, or even, for the foreman, announcing the verdict, but sitting afterwards hearing the previous circumstances of the defendant and the consequent sentence for him. In one jury where the trial had dragged on to mid-afternoon without a break for lunch and the jury had given their verdict, the judge said they could leave if they wished before the sentencing. Everybody had complained in the jury room of being hungry and tired but nobody moved. It was impossible to walk out of the court without hearing the sentence.

If all this gives an impression of confusion then that, in my experience, is fair. Jury service is a confusing experience. Jurors are told very little about what is going on. They are kept waiting around without much explanation for hours on end. They get the most cursory explanation of their duties and nobody ever mentions the existence of jury rules. They frequently receive only a partial account of the facts from the evidence and cross-examinations. Too frequently they get a less than adequate interpretation of the law from the judge. After all this they are shut in a room and asked to reach a decision of an excessively simple-minded nature – guilty or innocent – without regard to the character or much of the motivation of the defendant, and certainly in ignorance of the consequence to him of that decision.

In these circumstances what passes for discussion and decision-making in the jury room is also messy. A good summing-up from a judge is probably the greatest help a jury can have. An impartial résumé of the evidence to refresh the jury's memory and a clear and structured exposition of the legal issues are essential if the jury are to take the whole picture into account and not reach a verdict by focusing narrowly on one aspect of the case in an attempt to simplify choice. A good foreman is also a help if he can ensure that everybody has a say and that the issues set out by the judge are thoroughly and systematically discussed. Beyond that it is a matter of each juror doing his best according to his conscience.

What actually happens in the jury room seems to be a matter of widespread curiosity, like initiation rites in Masonic lodges. In both cases the oath of silence and the secrecy enhance the mystery and make curiosity inevitable. What actually happens is that twelve assorted people with nothing much else in common other than their humanity and their presence there together for the duration discuss what they have heard and try to form a unanimous view of the matter. It is just a discussion, sometimes heated, mostly leisurely, but rarely a debate or a disputation. Most juries can come to unanimous opinions fairly easily. Only occasionally are marathon sessions needed to reach decisions. As with so many mysteries, at the heart there is a commonplace. What happens in the jury room is about the most unremarkable, probably because least formalized, aspect of court procedures.

Nevertheless, many people seem to find the jury room experience genuinely distressing. In the case of trials which lasted over to the next day, some jurors admitted to having had sleepless nights, not racked by uncertainty so much as burdened by the responsibility. The housewives in particular seemed to find it hard. For some people their lives, particularly their working lives, accustom them to making decisions which effectively mean passing judgment on others, often to their detriment: teachers passing or failing examinees, managers hiring or firing employees, bureaucrats conferring or withholding benefits of one kind or another. For such people the juror's duty is fairly familiar: to understand the evidence, apply the rules and reach a decision as best as one can, accepting the possibility of misjudgment. But for others, women as housewives, unskilled workers, eighteen-year-olds in their first jobs, it is a new and understandably unwelcome responsibility. Some people could hardly bring themselves to utter the word 'guilty' even within the secrecy of the jury room. Most people thought the worst thing about being foreman was having to announce the verdict in open court.

And yet, it is the very representativeness of the jury that justifies its existence as an amateur element in the otherwise professionalized court procedures. If one's prime reaction to the jury service experience is to reinforce one's intention never to find oneself in the defendant's box, then one's second main reaction is to give thanks that it is to a jury that the decision of one's guilt or innocence would be entrusted. Rather that than putting oneself solely at the mercy of the police, the judge or the barristers, however benign they may be. Oddly, I had always thought beforehand that the jury as an institution was designed principally to spare the judiciary from the responsibility of determining guilt, by spreading that responsibility among a large number of unidentifiable citizens. It now seems to me that its prime function is the opposite: to spare the defendant from the judiciary by making him subject to the judgment of his fellows in all their ignorance and knowledge, clearsightedness and confusion, folly and wisdom, but above all humanity.

Penelope Wallace

I have now served on a jury on three separate occasions, and once as a 'shadow' juror in connection with a report being prepared by the Oxford University Penal Research Unit. My career, however, was almost stillborn since, on the first occasion – at the Oxford Assize Court, as it then was – I was one of the spares and not called upon.

When discharged, I inquired whether I should be summoned on a future occasion and was told that I shouldn't. I said that was a pity and the surprised official announced that if I actually *wanted* to be on a jury, he would make sure that my name was kept on the list.

I don't know what makes people like myself anxious to serve on a jury; partly, I suppose, a selfish desire to be involved in a dramatic event, partly an egotistic belief that one has something to contribute.

My first actual service, at the Oxford Quarter Sessions in the late 'sixties, was held before a Recorder and lacked the pageantry I had seen at the Assizes. The court room itself, in the nineteenth-century Town Hall, is dark with wood panelling and the jurors' benches were designed to keep the jury awake. In addition to the usual hardness of uncovered wood, these benches are so narrow that the slightest relaxation has the juror on the floor. The cases were fairly routine: the first defendant accused of stealing tyres for his car; the second of obtaining goods by false pretences.

Although pedestrian in type, both cases were interesting for different reasons. The first because the defendant's original explanation to the police had been that the tyres were on the car when he bought it so that the prosecution evidence was solely concerned to prove that those tyres were not available at the time the car was purchased. At no time did the prosecution attempt to prove that the tyres came from the factory where he worked or that they couldn't have been obtained elsewhere. In court the defendant changed his story and said he had purchased the tyres later and despite a certain vagueness as to his supplier, on the evidence presented, we eventually found him not guilty.

On the first ballot eight thought the defendant guilty and four not guilty. All had failed to notice during the case that the prosecution hadn't called any evidence to prove where the tyres came from but one juror maintained that the judge had mentioned this omission in his summing-up; we therefore returned to the court so that the foreman might ask the Recorder to repeat that portion of his advice.

On this jury I was the only woman and was referred to by the jury foreman as 'madam juror'. I discovered a surprising fact; namely that the chance composition of a jury – twelve randomly chosen people – covers an incredibly wide stratum of knowledge and experience. In this case, the defendant said his hobby was panel-beating. 'A skilled job,' we said, 'not connected with his work at the factory; an unlikely story.' 'No,' said one juror, 'I am a radiographer and my spare-time occupation is panel-beating.' You'd never get away with that in fiction.

The second day we had a defendant who said he had been asked to build bungalows. He didn't know where the sites were and he'd never seen them; but he'd met this man in a pub and, on the strength of the meeting, he'd gone to the local supplier, ordered and collected two hand-drills and twenty gallons of white paint to be entered to his non-existent account.

The jury on the first count split eight:four in favour of a Guilty verdict. Eventually eleven of us agreed he was guilty, the twelfth obstinately insisting – people who disagree with oneself tend to be labelled 'obstinate' – that it might be the first blot on a hitherto innocent record.

To me, this is woolly thinking; it is the duty of the jury to decide the defendant's guilt or otherwise and it is for the judge to evaluate the blot against any previous innocence – after all, most murderers are first offenders. We subsequently discovered that this particular defendant had a spotty past of thirty years' petty wrong-doing and one could only wonder why he hadn't learnt from dire experience to think up a more likely story.

The only worry I had about that case was that the twelfth man became converted while I was in the Ladies and I think it would be a good idea if the jury were to cease discussing a case during temporary absences; furthermore we retired to deliberate at lunchtime – with only tea and biscuits provided – and I think calm reason rather than starvation should bring about unanimity. Perhaps statutory hours of work and meal breaks could be introduced.

Incidentally, it was during the case of the man with the small hand-drills that I experienced a superb example of the British Temperament; the fire alarm clanged and the fire engine sirens brayed through the open window. Nobody moved. Fortunately it was a false alarm . . .

It was shortly after this that the Oxford University Penal Research Unit asked me to serve on a 'shadow jury'. In 1968 this Unit, then directed by the Oxford Reader in Criminology (who is now the Wolfson Professor of Criminology in Cambridge) set up a study of contested trials. This was financed by the Home Office and carried out by Mrs Sarah McCabe and Mr Robert Purves.

In the U.S.A. the Chicago Jury Project had been studying the jury's effectiveness; there was also growing socio-legal interest in this country and, shortly before the study was started, the Association of Chief Police Officers – prompted by Sir Robert Mark, then Chief Constable of Leicester – published in the *New Law Journal* acquittal rates for trials in higher courts.

In an attempt to find out how a jury might reach its verdict it was decided to select members of the public eligible for jury service and to ask them to act as a 'shadow' or second jury; to sit in the public gallery during a case and deliberate elsewhere at the same time as the real jury, the vital difference being that, when the shadow jury debated their verdict, they were tape-recorded.

What struck me most forcibly about this experiment was the complete lack of corporate identity of the shadow jury. We were twelve people; we remained twelve people – individual and in no way part of a whole. Perhaps this was partly because of the short time we were together but I believe it is the importance and seriousness of the task, the dramatic impact, which welds a real jury into an entity; as doctors and nurses forget personal enmities during an operation, so the jury at a trial becomes a team.

My second stint was back at the Assizes which, by then, had become the Crown Court; in fact the first session after the 1971 Courts Act came into effect. Here was greater activity than at the Town Hall, for there were two courts and a W.R.V.S. lady with a tea-trolley so that the entrance hall had a friendly atmosphere with jurors, witnesses, defendants not in custody, solicitors and barristers all rubbing shoulders.

Since a juror must be circumspect and since my first uncalled visit had revealed the total impossibility of judging who was who – the criminal-looking youths had all turned out to be law students, and the dear old lady with the knitting had bashed her husband on the head with a lump of metal – it behoved the juror to speak to no one except the tea-lady.

Here the second court – normally the council chamber – was light and airy and the jury sat in comfortable leather chairs. As the case involved dangerous driving and there were a number of maps and photographs to study, a degree of comfort was extremely welcome.

At the end of this case, the jury did not have an immediate ballot. I think we all felt that the defendant was guilty but wanted to discuss the case thoroughly before saying so.

The last time I served on a jury was in 1972 at the Old Bailey – I was called there as I have a small flat in London. Here there is no mingling; everything is geared to the dispensing of justice. Jurors have their own cloakrooms and their own excellent and cheap canteen. Thirty judges sit in as many courts – overflowing into the Law Courts in the Strand when necessary; but I didn't find that this large-scale operation detracted from the friendliness of the officials who were concerned at bringing me up from Oxford and who put me on a short-term jury comprising people who were shortly going on holiday. The attitude to jurors' needs is extremely reasonable and, where a case is thought likely to last for a long time, they are warned in advance.

The most impressive part of the Old Bailey jury service is the actual calling. In a great painted room two hundred jurors wait on benches for their names to be read out. Impressive and a little frightening; perhaps because it evokes a memory of doctors' waiting rooms, a hospital, scenes of those who wait in vain for visas to escape.

I felt nothing dramatic when my name was called because I never use my first Christian name, so each time it took me a while to respond. On the first occasion, the outcome was a quick march down Fleet Street to the Law Courts. I am not an athletic type and my moans that I was here to be a juror and not to compete in the Marathon fell on deaf ears since I trailed the field. I do think a small minibus would be helpful on these occasions. Furthermore, subsequent sessions were held in different courts at the Old Bailey and I don't think this shuffle while a case is proceeding is particularly helpful to judge, jury or anyone else concerned.

When this particular jury was sworn in, one juror had the greatest difficulty with the oath, in reading or even repeating it; yet that same man drew our attention to something in the written evidence which none of us had noticed. The case concerned perjury arising from a driving offence and there was little doubt in any of the jurors' minds that the defendant was guilty – particularly after he had taken the stand!

Some of us were slightly apprehensive about the long sentence which seemed likely on such a charge, especially as there would have been no perjury had the magistrates checked the facts at the first trial. Had this happened the defendant would merely have been disqualified from driving – for defendants who plead not guilty at a trial and are then found guilty at the same trial do not normally face perjury charges. However, the judge was lenient; the man was fined and the jury was relieved.

I write crime fiction and I have always been interested in criminology – two interests inherited from my father – so I have been asked whether my experience of crime, fictitious and otherwise, made any difference to my experience as a juror. I imagine everybody takes something different to and from any experience. It is probable that every juror draws a slightly different conclusion from his experience of the system; but I believe that many will share mine.

I don't know whether I improved as a juror with each

additional experience because, before my first appearance, I was already familiar with court procedure since I had attended twice as a spectator. Moreover, I had seen trials in British films and on television and, although these are not always correct in every detail, they give the general impression. I might add that any connection between a fictional American court of justice and the British counterpart is purely imaginary – and I doubt whether it bears much resemblance to one in the States.

I don't think jurors are overawed by their surroundings; it would be an idea to invite them to attend a court as spectators before becoming an integral part of the proceedings – although many might begrudge the time.

Only on my first appearance was I the sole woman juror, but at no time did I feel any prejudice against me on that score. Besides, being on a jury is not a social occasion; most men are used to working with women and know that they are as capable as men. They are perfectly willing to listen to a woman if she talks sense – of course, if she doesn't, she will be condemned as a 'stupid woman' whereas a man will be 'stupid' without a noun. I believe it was James Agate who condemned women jurors by saying that no woman would believe another woman if she were wearing the wrong hat. I think the remark – like many witty generalizations – is totally untrue; women are just as capable of evaluating the evidence of other women as men are.

Recently there have been suggestions that juries in general are finding too many crooks not guilty; the complaints are stemming, quite naturally, from certain members of the police. There is evidence that the statistics quoted are sometimes misleading but undoubtedly many guilty people do go free after a jury trial and the reasons are fairly simple.

Jurors are not sentimentalists – as some believe – but they understand that the burden of proof is on the prosecution. The jury is not asked to decide whether Mr X is a shocking liar and probably a thief. They are asked to decide whether the prosecution has proved that, on this occasion, there *was* a theft and Mr X was the one responsible. Even the suggestion that a prisoner's previous record should be disclosed to the jury would only show that Mr X is habitually a thief; it still won't prove he committed this particular crime – and may well arouse sympathy for the defendant on the assumption that the police are hounding him because of his past.

'Burden of proof' is an apt description. It must sometimes lie very heavily on the police on whom it primarily falls. This is because the British, fundamentally a just nation, have so circumscribed their police force with safeguards for the guilty that it surprises me that so many cases do actually reach the courts. It doesn't surprise me, however, that some are inadequate and I think we should stop treating the detection of crime as some sort of game – so that a criminal's confession is inadmissable unless the detective has first thrown a double six, and the prosecution must put their cards on the table while the defendant can play his 'close to the chest'. Even in games the rules are usually the same for both players; and the police must be given equal rights if they are to produce the evidence on which justice may be done.

If the jury is to render a true verdict then it must be allowed to evaluate *all* the evidence – however it is acquired. I do not, of course, suggest we condone any kind of police brutality. I am also aware of the danger of invasion of privacy, but wouldn't most people prefer to have their house searched tidily by the local police than gone over regularly and roughly by the neighbourhood burglar?

The next step between the police evidence and the jury is the presentation in court and here we come to the prosecution barrister and the legal backing. It is interesting to compare the fifty-per-cent acquittal rates in the higher courts in general against the rate in cases prosecuted by the Director of Public Prosecution, which is only thirteen per cent.

There would be two reasons for this. Cases referred to the D.P.P. include murder, attempted murder, rape, obscene and indecent libels, and sex offences against children; all crimes with which the public – and therefore the jury – have little sympathy.

In less serious crimes, sympathy is traditionally with the counsel for the defence and, illogically, whereas a good defence barrister will arouse sympathy for his client, the client will not necessarily lose sympathy if his counsel is unconvincing.

Thankfully, the days of great rhetoric have passed; the public no longer appreciates bear-baiting or the bullying of witnesses, nor the wit of good education against an illiterate man. A barrister must be a psychologist and, when he addresses the jury, he must have that sense which enables him to gauge their reactions as he tries to make them see the case through his eyes and thus through the eyes of his client.

There is nothing wrong in a barrister defending a man he believes guilty – for he could be wrong. It is for the jury to decide whether the defendant is guilty or not.

So everything is in favour of counsel for the defence, but why is counsel for the prosecution often so hopeless? Is it a matter of conscience? The responsibility for a man's future on the one hand against a feeling that 'if we don't get him for this we'll get him for something else'?

At the old Quarter Sessions, I heard the prosecution counsel refer sneeringly to the defendant's claim that he had bought some tyres from a certain firm 'obviously inventing the firm's name on the spur of the moment since it resembled the name of the police officer who was questioning him'. Yet any fool – including counsel – could open a telephone directory and see that the firm did exist, and sold tyres; its name was unusual but not fictitious.

Which brings me to the subsidiary reason for the D.P.P.'s lower acquittal rate. For the courts at the Old Bailey he has first lien on Treasury Council – appointed by the Attorney General and consisting of seven seniors and four juniors; in other courts he has barristers appointed for the case by the A.G. and to prepare the case he has a professional legal staff of more than fifty. Other cases are now handled by the local police authority's legal department and the prosecuting barrister is appointed for the case by that police authority. There are now forty-three police authorities in England and Wales and each has a legal department of up to twenty. In fairness, it should be stated that force amalgamation to create these larger police authorities – warranting their own legal department – is comparatively recent. Whereas the old system, sometimes with help from the town clerk's legal staff, might once have been adequate it became totally inadequate with the increased number of trials at higher courts. This increase is partly due to the general rise of crime rates and partly due to the fact that, under the 1967 Criminal Justice Act, magistrates now accept written evidence in more serious cases and send it to a higher court without considering or even reading it themselves – provided that the defendant is legally represented and his representative raises no objection. Thus, cases which might formerly have been dealt with by magistrates are now passed on.

It is difficult to ascertain what percentage of cases before a jury are prosecuted by the D.P.P.; his department handles ten to twelve per cent of indictable cases in England and Wales but not all of these come before a jury, some being dealt with summarily by a magistrate. The D.P.P. also handles two to three per cent of summary cases. (In 1966 the D.P.P. prosecutions numbered 3,300 out of 1,500,000; less than 1 in 450.) Even if we were to give the D.P.P. a ten per cent prosecution rate in jury cases, this still leaves ninety per cent to be handled by the police legal departments.

It seems to me that jurors have a perfect right to criticize the system since they are the only unpaid participants – except for the defendant – present throughout the trial. A juror wishes to render a true verdict for which he requires *all* the evidence, lucidly presented, from both sides.

It often surprised me that barristers had so much latitude. At one court, in Oxford, counsel for the defence on this occasion requested a policeman to check certain points on the condition of the road which were totally irrelevant since, in the months which had elapsed between the accident and the trial, the state of the road was likely to have changed. At the Old Bailey trial, defence counsel made his final speech in the teeth of his client's evidence in the box – a difficult task made more so, one would think, by the fact that the prosecution barrister was chatting and laughing with his junior throughout. One expected a stern voice to call for silence.

I heard of another surprising occurrence at a multi-jury court. One of the jurors admitted that she knew the defendant; she was removed from that jury and put on another but apparently was not cautioned to silence for, during the lunch break, she regaled the first jury with the defendant's earlier record.

I have already mentioned the trial at the Old Bailey when the defendant's alleged perjury followed his appearance at a Magistrates' Court charged with exceeding the speed limit. His defence then was that his car had been stolen and that, at the moment he was supposed to be committing the crime, his car was in someone else's hands. He stated – which was true – that he had reported the theft to the police who had later found and returned his car. The magistrates accepted his explanation. However, it subsequently transpired that the theft and return took place some while before the speeding offence and I should have thought it sensible for the magistrates to check this evidence with the police before reaching a decision; thus saving police and jury time, and the cost of a case at the Old Bailey.

I also believe that the constitution of the jury itself needs some adjustment. Since early 1974 jurors have been drawn from the whole electoral roll and not from those recorded as house-holders, thus enabling more women and a broader stratum of people to be called upon – broader both as to age and income.

There has always been criticism about the educational standards of juries, but this is surely ridiculous. Centuries have passed since the business of the court was conducted in Latin and, when legal terminology is used – and it is possible to be well educated without being learned in law – it is explained to the court. Perforce the language is clear and simple since the defendant, in my experience, is rarely a highly educated man – cynics might say that, if he were, he wouldn't have been apprehended.

So there is no problem over communication. Is there any difficulty in understanding the nature of the crime, evaluating the evidence, judging the reliability of witnesses? It is acknowledged that higher education does not necessarily equate with intelligence. Most crimes are perfectly understood by all sections of the community and people are usually capable of deciding whether or not a witness is lying.

I say *most* crimes because I think there are exceptions, when a general jury is inadequate. I do not agree with the practice of excluding women from juries dealing with certain sex crimes. Women have never been more squeamish than men and it has ceased to be fashionable for them to appear so. No doubt the defence would believe them likely to be more sensitive in cases of child ill-usage but facts of recent baby battering do not seem to bear out this theory. There are individuals, both women and men, who are particularly upset by cases of this sort and they should be excused service on such a jury; otherwise women should be included.

The crimes which are most difficult for a general jury are those where a certain particularized knowledge is required: fraud, for example. Many frauds are perpetrated in the City, because more opportunities occur there. Scotland Yard has a special 'Fraud Squad'. In the days when the Old Bailey jurors were drawn from a smaller section of London, there was probably a fairly high percentage of accountants among them; but these days the catchment area is enormous and such a jury would be lucky to include one accountant – and in this case he would be likely to have a disproportionate voice in proceedings. At such trials, therefore, the composition of the jury should perhaps be more selective.

However, there are many occasions where a large area from which jurors may be called would make for better justice. For example, in Oxford, a high proportion of the residents work at a local factory and from time to time jurors and defendants from there may be included in the same cases. Thus, if a man is accused of theft from the factory, such jurors, knowing from experience that these thefts are prevalent, will find it easier to believe the defendant's guilt. Additionally, in a small area, there is a greater possibility that a juror will know the record or reputation of a defendant or be prejudiced by the area in which he lives.

Further conclusions I have reached as a result of jury experience are that ex-policemen and ex-members of the legal profession should be barred from jury service since they may have previous knowledge of the defendant. I know of one case where an ex-policeman juror actually recognized the prisoner as a man with a criminal record; although he kept silence until after the jury had given their verdict.

Any documents produced for study by the jury should be very carefully vetted beforehand lest they contain information which the prosecution would not be allowed to produce in court: for example, photocopies of a driving licence showing previous convictions which, if two are shown, provides an excellent motive for avoiding a third with the certainty of disqualification.

Since my last jury appearance, I have learnt that the jury may interrupt a case and ask the judge to put questions to the witnesses or defendant and it is surely very important that this right should be made clear to the jury before the trial begins.

Some members of the police force believe that juries deliberate darkly, mysteriously and inexplicably but I am sure that many jurors would be happy after the trial to pass on their comments; to tell the police where they think the prosecution case was inadequate from the jury's point of view. However, any such exchange would have to be very carefully organized – preferably through a third party who would not disclose the identity of the individual juror – for, in these days of increased possibilities of breaking the law, most of us are at risk and Joe Bloggs, juror, is not going to tell the police that he personally voted against their case lest that same force should search more diligently for *his* illegally parked car, *his* cigarette packet thrown from the window, *his* dog fouling the pavement.

Certainly let us have research into the jury system of criminal justice. However, since the days of Athens, where the jury system and democracy virtually began, one has always been synonomous with the other. Sometimes it has been misused, as in 1670 when twelve jurors were shut up without food for two nights, and subsequently fined and imprisoned, because they would not bring in the Guilty verdict called for. This incident is commemorated by a plaque at the Old Bailey, and a descendant of one of the twelve is now a High Court judge of the Chancery Division; ironically, there are no juries in this division.

A free jury guarantees that a defendant's culpability is decided by twelve people, who, to the best of their ability, thoughtfully weigh the evidence; twelve people who are not intimidated by judge or barrister, police or politicians. Like democracy itself, the jury system may have faults, but it is impossible to envisage a better one.

Alan Wykes

First impressions first. 'Bewildered,' I recorded in my notebook. 'Reported ten-fifteen at Shire Hall as summoned. Stood about in vast foyer till ten-thirty. Usher called the roll. All present – some forty of us. Pep-talk about importance of job. Divided into two parties – one for Crown Court and one for *Nisi Prius* Court. Told to wait in foyer till called. Much coming and going of witnesses and barristers. Sudden silence called for by policeman. Main doors to street opened, enter judge's procession: senior police officers, his honour in scarlet, two Harrods-type ladies, an apparent Lord Lieutenant or High Sheriff. Procession disappeared into Crown Court, doors shut, thin spring sunshine vanished from tessellated floor of foyer – which, judging by markings, does secondary duty as squash court. Five minutes later another call for silence; but no procession this time, the judge being of lowlier degree – a Recorder in fact. Black gown flapping he crossed to the *Nisi Prius* Court and disappeared therein. Asked pretty, mini-skirted usher (usherette?), "*Nisi prius* . . . unless before *what*?" Her response uninformed: "Something old-fashioned I think. Something to do with deportation would it be?" '

It wouldn't. Later, I looked up the answer for myself. Like so much legal hocus-pocus it's lost its meaning (which was originally to do with the specific Court of Westminister) along the centuries and has no special significance nowadays. In any case, as we were to learn, the hearing of cases is not confined to the designated court rooms. The scene is shifted as required to outbuildings mysteriously known as Terrapins, to Council chambers, and anonymous rooms in the Town Hall. Accommodation, it seems, doesn't keep up with the pressure of business. With the population exploding all round us crime naturally explodes too. There aren't enough barristers, ushers, clerks, or places to put them all in.

Nor, as I was also to learn, is there enough information about court procedure given in the pamphlet accompanying the summons to attend. Since the average citizen's lifelong concern is to keep out of courts of law, a précis of the British legal system could prevent many irrelevant questions arising in the juror's mind when he's supposed to be concentrating his attention on judge, counsel or witnesses. Instead, one goes to court with vague and inaccurate notions which in my own case were further muddled by inaccurate interpretations of procedure perpetrated by court officials.

But first the ideas one has grown up with which turned out to be accurately reflected in the happenings I experienced.

I've always cherished the thought that alleged wrongdoers are tried by their peers rather than by 'gentry' (if such exist nowadays); that juries are a real cross section of the community; that no one outside a few exempted professions can escape service except on account of illness; and that since enfranchisement of women they too are liable for their stint. All those notions were supported by my experience.

I'd certainly have welcomed exemption, for although new experience should in theory always be welcome to a writer, in practice it isn't so welcome when you have to chip a fortnight out of a book's time allotment and know it'll take you six weeks to get back into the rhythm of the word wagon. I craftily suggested that perhaps I was too well known to be a good choice for a juryman. True, mine is not a name that leaps to everybody's mind when asked to name a living writer; but I'm certainly quite well known in Reading, where I live, as the historian of both the town and its police force; and I've often been agreeably astonished to find that I'm not unrecognized, anyway as a name, among the general reading public elsewhere. But local notoriety didn't exempt me.

As for the three juries I served on during my three weeks, they seemed to be a fair cross section – as regards occupation anyway. They included two clerks, a grocery assistant, a cinema cashier, a builder's foreman, a couple of teachers (one of them a headmaster), three housewives (all three were selected for one of the cases we tried, so anyone who says it's rare to find more than one woman on a jury isn't supported by me), a race-course tipster, a taxi driver, a sub-editor, a shop manager and a waiter. I doubt if a section of the community could be much more crossed than that. Also, I doubt if any of them – certainly not me – could be classed as 'gentry'. I'd say that we were all the 'equal in standing and rank' (which is what peer means) of those brought to trial before us.

We'd been warned that we *mustn't talk to any recognizable acquaintances* ('Even your own families,' the usher who'd called the roll warned us solemnly) who happened to appear in the environs of the court. I checked afterwards and found that what he should have told us was *not to discuss the case* with people we knew. I was slightly and irrelevantly alarmed that I should have to ignore my wife if she chanced to pass Shire Hall as I was entering or emerging – as she was quite likely to do on her way to the lunchtime concert at the Town Hall. (Even more alarming was the possible permanence of the embargo – 'What, never to talk to anyone I know again?') The shop manager, whom I'd chummed up with to relieve the boredom of hanging about waiting to be called, told me that several young men ascending to the public gallery were customers of his; and indeed nods of recognition were exchanged. But lips were sealed. A feeling of real importance was shared among all of us. We genuinely believed that nothing must bias us in our consideration of the cases to be paraded before us. Even among ourselves we conversed in whispers; and when we went our different ways for lunch and reassembled at the appointed hour (it was always precisely an hour allowed by the court) we shyly spoke of matters of everyday concern, repressing with conscientious fervour anything to do with the case under consideration. We did not want to be influenced by our fellow jurors' thoughts. There was, as I checked afterwards, a genuine concern that unanimity of verdict should be arrived at individually.

But that was way ahead. On our first day, having done nothing at all in the furtherance of justice, we were dismissed at lunchtime and told to report at ten-fifteen next morning, Tuesday. We did so, eager for the drama; but again there was nothing for us before lunch and it was two-forty-five before twelve of us were actually selected – but only to be gathered together and bellwethered by yet another usher through a maze of underground passages to a prefabricated Terrapin on the outskirts of the town centre, where we heard the clerk read the indictment and were sworn in without challenge. But some other case had priority and the Recorder apologetically dismissed us again till next day.

'However, you've heard the indictment, have been sworn in without challenge, and we can get straight on with the case at eleven-fifteen tomorrow morning, ladies and gentlemen of the jury. Thank you very much.'

There's a lot heard about the peremptory challenge, a recent innovation – if innovation it is. This gives the accused the right to challenge up to seven of the twelve jurors without giving any reason. But no challenges came our way; and it struck me it would be difficult to get one in anyway. The clerk to the court simply told the prisoner that if he wished to challenge he must do so before 'he [the juror] comes to be sworn'; by which time the juror already has the Testament in his right hand (what exactly is so sacred about the right hand?) and is reading the oath off the card. Presumably, I thought, the wilier birds know what's coming and slip in the challenge quickly. I subsequently discovered that challenges are normally made by counsel (unless the defendant is defending himself); but as I've shown, in my case the invitation to challenge was vague enough (possibly through over familiarity on the clerk's part) to give me a totally false impression. Evidently there were challenges in courts other than those in which I was present, for there were some disgruntled jurors hanging about from time to time. 'Saucy sod. He challenged me, no reason, I've never seen the chap in my life. Just delaying tactics if you ask me.'

We'd had enough delaying tactics ourselves, but there were no complaints that I heard. Evidently we'd all taken seriously the apologia in the pamphlet accompanying our summons: 'Since it's not always possible to forecast accurately when a particular case will start or how long it will last, persons called for jury service will sometimes find themselves waiting at the Court for what may seem an unnecessarily long time . . . when delay occurs, as it occasionally does, the patience and forbearance of jurors is much appreciated.'

So, patience and forbearance having prevailed over the irritations of the law's (unavoidable) delays, it was Wednesday of our first week before the twelve of us empanelled actually got to grips with our first case. The charge was one of gaining money by deception, and the accused were a middle-aged couple – the husband Polish with long residence in England but little talent in speaking the language; the wife with a long history of neurosis and mental illness, as defence counsel subtly emphasized. The prosecution's case was that the wife, having visited a betting shop to place a bet for her brother, had subsequently conspired with her husband (who had watched the race on T.V. and knew the horse had won) to pretend to the betting shop manager that her husband had also placed a bet on the same horse but that his receipt ticket had been lost. There's a routine to be gone through in the case of lost tickets. It was duly invoked and the husband was paid his supposed winnings. When the brother went later to claim he was naturally told the the cupboard was bare. Whereupon, eschewing brotherly love, he'd set the case against his sister and brother-in-law in motion.

Inevitably one makes subjective judgments of people in the limelight before one. How can one help classifying them to some extent by their clothes, demeanour, physiognomy? Then, realizing that, one correctively leans over backwards to rid oneself of spontaneous impressions – thereby acquiring a set of different, but equally subjective, notions. I can't speak for my fellow jurors, but I suspect that many of them felt initially as I did about the couple in the dock – that they looked pathetically bewildered – then firmly corrected that first impression so that they became transformed by the corrective process into a couple bent on deception. True, as the evidence unfolds one achieves a more regulated judgment and remembers that clothes *don't* make the man, that villains don't necessarily look villainous, and that hesitancy in replying to questions may be due simply to 'nerves'. But to me the first impressions remained to a large extent ineradicable.

The accused were well served by their counsel, a tall young man whose eloquence I admired while irrelevantly wondering who paid his fees if the defendant couldn't. (Legal Aid? Friends? Public funds? Is there any reason jurors shouldn't be told this inessential but interesting bit of information?) And as the case unfolded I fell to wondering, equally irrelevantly, what would happen if one of the witnesses turned out to be Jewish and wanted to take the oath on the Old Testament. There seemed to be no provision: all the Testaments were New and the clerk made no offer to accommodate the Judaic faith or, for that matter, atheists, Catholics, Hindus or Moslems, none of whom can be said to be thin on the ground these days. Presumably, I thought, they all have to nip in quickly, just as I'd supposed the accused has to if he wants to challenge a juror. But I subsequently checked with a Jewish friend of mine, a doctor often called on to give medical evidence. He told me he always takes his Swearing Kit with him – an Old Testament and a beret. I also learnt, when the wish for the knowledge had passed, that witnesses who wish to affirm or swear on the Catholic missal or in any other way have to notify the court usher, who asks the judge's permission. But how can witnesses know this if they're not told in advance or at the time? And how many of them feel free to lie like Ananias because they haven't sworn on the symbol of their particular faith?

As witnesses went through counsel's hoops many more irrelevant thoughts impinged. How does anyone in the public gallery hear what's going on when it's not all that easy to hear soft-voiced replies even when you're not more than a few yards from them in the well of the court? Presumably it's unimportant, since trial by jury is a matter of truth-seeking, not public entertainment. But the reporters weren't much better placed – though they rewardingly had a much better view of the distractingly pretty shorthand-writer recording the proceedings (often referred to by the Recorder, when trying to straighten out slurred speech and off-track answers, as 'Madam Shorthand-Writer'). The press reports I read afterwards were not exactly a travesty of the proceedings; but they'd suffered much in transcription – possibly more at sub-editors' hands than from the inaudibility of witnesses.

The prosecution's case got off to a bad start because of the zealousness of the police officer who'd interviewed the defendants. He'd extracted from them statements that were virtual admissions of guilt, which for a moment seemed to make the prosecution's case cut, dried and polished. But under cross-examination, asked what he did directly after getting the statements signed he used the unfortunate phrase, 'I made up my notes.'

'You *made them up?*' defence counsel asked with subtle incredulity.

'Well, I mean, I wrote them down.'

'Ah. It's rather different, isn't it?'

But the phrase had stuck – in my mind if in no one else's. One knew perfectly well that he hadn't made them up in the sense of concocting them; but as with the impinging irrelevancies of demeanour and physiognomy an ineradicable impression was left. Equally, when the first defendant came to the witness box subjective impressions over-rode what surely should have been objective considerations of fact. Surely the man's comprehension of the questions put to him was as limited as his command of English? Could he possibly have understood, let alone used, the idiomatic English in the statement the policeman had put before him to sign? There even came a point at which the Recorder thought an interpreter might have to be called in. (Selfishly I began to consider how long an adjournment might be necessary, whether seeking an interpreter might extend my spell of jury service by days.) But gradually questions were threaded into the linguistically slow mind and answers were squeezed out, while the defendant's hands whitened as they gripped the top of the witness box.

When his wife was called she had to be helped into the box, then helped out again as the Recorder ordered that she should be given a chair nearer the jury so that her whispered, uncomprehending replies could be heard. Could it possibly be that this simple-minded soul had been a conspirator in such a complex design as had been spread before us? (And it was truly complex, with its betting shop jargon and its confusing spread of bets that always seemed to have too little money backing too many horses.) I had a personal answer to that. I knew that it could be. Some years ago I wrote a definitive book on gambling and I established that the gambling mentality has little to do with I.Q. Nor, for that matter, is language any barrier to the understanding of betting subtleties. An Andaman Islander with a gambling mind but otherwise sub-normal mentally could comprehend the complexities of the Tote in two minutes flat, even if he'd never seen one in his life. In natural gamblers a stratum of the mind can be richly ored with the esoterica of gambling at the expense of every other endowment.

Whether this was understood by the prosecution I don't know; but nothing was made of it. So compassion, inspired mainly by the pathetic bewilderment of the defendants, won. To me, the prosecution lost out on two points: the evidence of an over-zealous policeman and the failure to call technical evidence that might have convinced us that, sadly dim and uncomprehending though the defendants were, they would still have been capable of the alleged conspiracy. But one finds on the evidence. We found Not Guilty.

Next morning we faced a case of a very different kind: alleged obstruction of the railway to the danger of the passengers. I don't know if everybody else's hackles rose at hearing the charge; mine certainly did. Here, I assumed, was one of those wretched people who for some kind of kick fling blocks of concrete on to the rails. I'd practically decided, surreptitiously, on a verdict of Guilty even before we entered the jury box and were sworn in. But the wording of a charge spreads over wide ground. The accused, an apparently law-abiding young man (impressions again: how can one possibly judge rectitude by a suit of clothes, a tidy haircut, and an upright manner?) was alleged to have driven his car over a level-crossing without asking the controlling signal box for permission. Madness, it appeared; maybe even criminal madness. But as the story was in turn blown up and deflated it was seen to be divisible into two parts of equal triviality.

At the location in question, a narrow lane having no other purpose than to give access to a couple of cottages crossed the railway. At the time of the alleged offence the young man had lived in one of the cottages for rather less than a month. Long ago, residents of, or visitors to, the cottages had simply walked across the line, it being considered their own affair if, having looked both ways up and down the line, they didn't give any approaching train the right of way. But with increasing and faster railway traffic, more sophisticated methods had prevailed and level-crossing gates had been installed. (They opened, incidentally, outward on to the road, not inward across the railway.) But because the road traffic remained limited to the few residents of the cottages and their callers the gates had always been manually operated, safety being ensured by a rule that required people using the road to telephone the nearest signal box to get the all-clear before opening the gates. This, according to the prosecution, the young man had not done on the date in question and the driver of an approaching train had seen him cross the railway in the path of the train, thus creating what might have been a dangerous situation had the driver not already been slowing down for a signal at danger.

The evidence included several exhibits for our consideration: there were photographs of the approach to the crossing along both road and railway, of the notice calling upon road users to call the signal box by using the roadside telephone conveniently provided by the management, British Rail, and of an older notice, never removed, calling upon them merely to Stop!! Look!! Listen!!; also of the signalman's logbook, which, at the hour in question, recorded no incoming call seeking clearance to open the gates. The signalman, an impressively stolid piece of British citizenry, held that there had been no such call. The young man's lady companion, however, said the call had been made and clearance given. The accused in the witness box added that in any case the driver had to stop because the signal was against him. That, counsel for the prosecution pointed out acidly, was nothing to do with it. Responsibility clearly lay with the road user and was defined in the notice requiring him to telephone the signal box. Equally acidly the young man replied that during his few weeks' residence he had complied – with increasing irritation since there were often delays in answering and equally often such vague answers as 'It's up to you,' were received. And anyway, what about the notice that merely required him to stop, look and listen?

At this point the Recorder, a genial Dickensian character who had sidetracked proceedings not inconsiderably by evincing a personal interest in the technical details of running a railway by asking signalman and train driver a good many questions that hadn't the slightest relevance to the case, said there would be a recess and told us, the jury, to have a jolly lunch.

If sausages and mash in a pub can be said to be jolly I had a jolly lunch and returned to pick up the threads, which during the afternoon worked themselves into a veritable cat's-cradle, with a parade of witnesses including a railway signalling engineer, telephone engineer, leading railman, the girlfriend, the girlfriend's father and the policeman who'd charged the accused – though whether in that order I can't remember. The concluding speeches by counsel pointed out, on the one side, the likelihood of the young man's irritation getting the better of him so often that in the end he simply didn't bother to use the telephone, and on the other the equal likelihood of the signalman having received the phone call and neglected to log it, it having been implied in evidence that other calls on the evening in question had also escaped the logbook. 'But is it likely,' prosecuting counsel rather hopefully added, 'that a signalman of this man's experience would neglect to keep his logbook up to date?' – only to be reminded by his learned friend on the other side that signalmen of experience were just as liable to human error as anyone else. We seemed bedazzled by erudition and evidence in a case in which a great deal of time and money had been spent to prove that (a) a notice had been ignored or (b) it hadn't or (c) the notice didn't have to be noticed anyway because there was another notice saying something different.

In his summing-up – an admirably lucid, concise, and perfectly balanced précis – the Recorder pointed out that it was for us to decide which was right – a premiss we could hardly doubt.

We were out ten minutes and acquitted the defendant. Some might have said we treated the case with scant attention out of contempt for its triviality. Others, on the other hand, might not.

The promising fascinations of a case of alleged forgery came next. The charge was a triple one: of stealing the cheque, of forging the owner's signature and of attempting to gain money by presenting it to the bank for payment. The accused, a free-lance chartered accountant, apparently (impressions again!) and according to his record of the highest degree of probity, had worked on the account books of the plaintiff. While doing so he was alleged to have made out a cheque for his own agreed fee and forged the plaintiff's signature on it – the plaintiff's contention being that he had already paid the fee in cash. The defence, of course, was that no payment had been made in cash and that the cheque was properly signed in settlement of the fee.

Once again there were a great many befogging circumstances introduced as evidence, including the revelation by the defence that the plaintiff was himself awaiting trial on charges of obtaining money by false pretences – which, together with his somewhat furtive appearance, could hardly fail to be a biasing factor. (I had innocently supposed that juries were not supposed to know anything to the discredit of the litigants; but such, obviously, is not the case.) For a time these fogs of Jarndyce obscured the nub of the matter – which, surely, was the alleged forgery. It was not disputed that the defendant had had access to the cheque book nor that he had made out cheques for the plaintiff to sign; it was the signature that was in dispute, the plaintiff averring vehemently that it was not his.

All of us, at that moment, cast our glances down to the photostat of the cheque with which we had been provided. There appeared to be no doubt that the signature was in a different hand from that which had written the payee's name, date and amount – which was not disputed as being the defendant's own writing. But if it was a forged signature that was to be expected. A forger's work is dedicated to deceiving by appearance. We sat back to await the testimony of some handwriting expert; but no such graphologist appeared. Indeed, in a case in which one would have supposed that expert evidence was above all essential there was none at all; and prosecuting counsel drew our attention to the fact – rather too gleefully, I thought – adding that we were by no means to take on ourselves the additional burden of assuming expertise in the interpretation of handwriting.

Whereupon, to my mind and no doubt to those of my fellow jurors, the rug was whisked away from under the case. How we could be expected to find a man guilty of forgery without expert opinion was a mystery. The prosecution had turned us into Swans bereft of Edgars, of Princeless Hamlets. We had little to go on but the 'Yes you did,' 'No I didn't' type of evidence. We acquitted again; whereupon defence counsel immediately asked for costs and got them. Whether that was a measure of the Recorder's agreement with our verdict I don't know.

What I do know is that in the last two cases with which we were concerned acquittals might have been less in doubt and our retirement time considerably more worthwhile if (a) in the level-crossing case we'd been more convinced of the need to prosecute at all and (b) in the cheque case we'd been supplied with what seemed essential evidence. The betting slip case was the most serious and the one to which we gave the longest and most justifiable consideration – in the most uncomfortable circumstances, incidentally. The only retiring room available was in another building, well away from the court, to which all of us were marched like a school crocodile with an usher at the head and a policeman at the tail (to see we weren't got at, presumably). It was an office filled with filing cabinets and a steel table on which several of us sat, there being no room for twelve chairs. Someone asked the usher who locked us in if there were any ashtrays. 'Use the waste bins,' he said. No one asked him about lavatory accommodation. Perhaps it was just as well.

Jury Bailiff

A jury bailiff is made and not born; the product of what we now call 'in-service training' and what the Chinese, it is alleged, call makee-learnee. He evolves, that is to say, through years of experience in the capacity (as a rule) of court usher and kindred duties. Jury bailiffs have always been men, and a growing number of them are now women, who are expected to combine the qualities of public guide, shepherd, friend and comforter in the job of marshalling and befriending their fellow-citizens called to jury service.

Mr Arthur Baldock, the senior jury bailiff at the Central Criminal Court (the Old Bailey), has three colleagues; two, as it happens, women. Between them they probably have the busiest jury bailiwick in Great Britain; and what keeps them busy is simply the administrative chore of recording and marshalling jurors and chasing up defaulters. Their jurors come, roughly 2,500 every month, from all the Home Counties and the City of London. Mr Baldock was first an usher at the Old Bailey and then at various times he worked as a clerk in the Court's administrative offices. You might suppose him, from his gown, to be an usher still, as he traverses the vast modern building which the new Old Bailey has become, but he is one no longer and has no authority over the ushers. He is occasionally waylaid by jurors seeking reassurance and advice; and it is likely to be the same kind of advice a myriad of times. It says much for the patience and job-satisfaction of Central Criminal Court jury bailiffs, who seem almost to be in a class apart, that they have a reputation for answering each all-too-familiar question as if it were being posed interestingly for the very first time.

When the juror-to-be receives his summons, he will find that it requires him to complete a form of reply. As this book was being written it still required him to say whether he had reached the age of sixty-five, that being the age beyond which neither men nor women are liable to serve. But while the system was changing over, which it could hardly do overnight, from the summoning of qualified ratepayers to the summoning of (almost) any elector between eighteen and sixty-five whether he pays rates or not, there was no practicable means by which the courts could discover his age. Accordingly 'on this occasion', said an accompanying *pro forma* letter from the jury summoning officer, 'the ages of persons to whom summonses have been sent are not known. If you have reached the age of sixty-five . . . I am sorry for any inconvenience caused to you by the receipt of these papers.' A newish note in the communication sent to jurors; to whom, in years gone by, the courts always adopted (on paper) the stern attitude implicit in the words 'herein fail not at your peril'.

The 'summoning officer' is in fact a firm of solicitors in Brentford High Street, acting for the Sheriff of London 'in the name of the Lord High Chancellor of Great Britain'. It is of the greatest importance that the summoning officer should be above suspicion, for a litigant has the right to object to the entire 'panel' (of 2,500 names or more) if he believes that they have not been disinterestedly selected; he can, to use the legal phrase, 'challenge the array'. It is a wildly unlikely event today, but in 1821 there occurred a case *(R. v. Dolly and Thelwall)* in which a publisher, charged with sedition, was able to prove that the sheriff who had summoned the jurors was a member of the association which had brought the prosecution. In the unlikely event of such a challenge today, its validity would have to be decided by two of the jurors who happened to attend for the 'ballot'.

The summoning officer also sends out a printed page of Information for Jurors, which tells them how to get to the Old Bailey, advises them not to bring cars, describes the hours of sitting and the average number of days involved, and says: *If in difficulty, ask for a jury bailiff.*

This preliminary correspondence completed, the summoning officer dispatches to the Old Bailey (monthly) a vast list of names and addresses – usually about 5,000. This document, known as 'the panel', was at one time beautifully inscribed on parchment and is now typewritten on sheets of cartridge paper about the size of a tabloid newspaper. Roughly half the names will have been crossed out because, on the strength of the information supplied by themselves, their owners have proved to be ineligible or disqualified for jury service; or because they are names of people who, though neither ineligible nor disqualified, have a right to be excused and have successfully claimed it. Among these 'persons entitled to be excused' are peers and peeresses; and they do not always claim excusal, either because they want to serve or (says Mr Baldock) because they forget – or perhaps don't even read the summons form. And this is why peers and peeresses are sometimes seen in the jury box, often to the mystification of observers who have supposed that peers are ineligible or disqualified. Nevertheless, people of that order of eminence are not frequently seen on juries, and Mr Baldock's interesting explanation of this justifies a digression.

If a man is well known to the public, the reason is likely to be that his membership of one of the professions or callings listed as 'ineligible for jury service' is the very thing that has brought him into the public eye. But there is one huge profession whose members are not ineligible, not disqualified, and not excusable as of right, and that is what is now known as the entertainment industry. Yet its members are seldom seen on juries. Why?

Mr Baldock explains that, in the words of the jury summons itself, *anyone* may, 'at the discretion of the Jury Summoning Officer, be excused on grounds such as illness, physical disability, insufficient understanding of English [which you might expect to be a ground for ineligibility rather than claimed excusal] or *for any other good reason*.' Such other good reason might be that an actor, a musician or a concert artist is in the middle of a play-run, a repertory season, or a series of engagements and will suffer heavy financial loss if made to serve. The maximum 'compensation for loss of earnings' payable under the Jurors' Allowances Regulations (as distinct from fares and expenses) is now £6.70 a day, which becomes £13.00 a day from the tenth day of continuous service on one trial; which may seem a low ceiling for a business tycoon, but which, if you recall the days when no juror, rich or poor, was paid anything, does at least tilt the balance in favour of the relatively poor man on juries rather than the rich. Excusal on these grounds is excusal for one session only, a mere postponement. But although there are actors who have been excused time after time, recent Old Bailey jurors have included Ian Carmichael, Ann Shelton and Ian Lavender (on leave from *Dad's Army*). Eric Morecambe was recently excused because of a long-running summer engagement with Ernie Wise; but not on the ground that he might, on occasion, distract attention by lifting his spectacles to shoot glances round the court room. In 1950 Professor Harold Laski was called for Old Bailey jury service, and applied for excusal time after time; obviously, it seemed to the court, in the utmost determination that he should never be made to serve. It may have seemed that Laski's well-known regard for constitutionality and the involvement of the ordinary citizen in the machinery of justice was a vicarious state of mind, a desire satisfied by the involvement of others. He went on resisting by every means he could devise. And in the end he won; after a series of deferments he died before he could be made to serve.

Mr Baldock has known a few cases in which reluctant jurors have carried their objections to the point of total defiance. What happens to such a man? If, for the sake of a quiet life (or a busy but uncomplicated life), the law washed its hands of him and let him go, he would soon have imitators. There must be a sanction. In a recent Old Bailey instance, a man resolutely declined to serve, refused to pay the £100 fine, and went off to Brixton Prison for three days. Not that the three days' imprisonment absolves him from jury service on a future occasion. He may, it is true, be thought to have established himself as a person not likely to make the best of jurors, and the jury bailiffs have long memories; but he will have paid a high price, if he proves thus to be immune, for a kind of immunity which few will envy him.

Let us, however, return to the 'panel', the jurors whose names survive on the much-amended monthly list. For each of these the Central Criminal Court receives from the summoning officer a yellow card, about half postcard-size, bearing the juror's name and address *only*. (Until January 1974 it recorded also his occupation; this was discontinued by direction of the Lord Chancellor because there had been instances in which a knowledge of jurors' occupations had imperilled the long-established principle of 'random selection'.) The 'panel' and its accompanying cards are the apparatus for a 'ballot', a drawing of lots. The 2,500-odd cards are put face-downwards in a large wooden tray (as many as possible at a time) and then shuffled. Under the supervision of the Court Administrator, the jury bailiff withdraws them in batches of sixteen (the four extras in each case to be available as reserves against last-minute illness or other defection), and each batch of sixteen is put into a separate envelope. This operation will usually produce more than 150 groups, which are then (in their envelopes) divided among the twenty-seven courts which make up the Old Bailey today.

By the Courts Act of 1971 (Section 32), anybody who is 'a party to the proceedings' has a right – *before the end of the trial* but not afterwards – to see the panel from which the jurors are to be drawn; and so has anyone 'acting on his behalf'. The court can, in addition, allow the same facility to anyone else, at its sole discretion. It is sometimes said that this arrangement, by providing addresses, makes it possible for anyone interested to make an unlawful approach to a juror; and it has been urged that even a litigant and his advisers should have access to the panel *only* on the day when the trial begins. But at the Old Bailey, at least, anyone so minded could gain only the roughest idea as to where in the Home Counties any juror might come from; he could merely furnish himself, if he had the time, with about 2,500 names and addresses, of which 2,500 minus sixteen (and he couldn't know which sixteen) would be totally irrelevant to his unlawful intentions.

The ballot should, to comply with the law, be conducted 'in open court', that is to say with the public in attendance. But, Mr Baldock points out, it is one of the weaknesses of any law requiring that something be done 'in public' or 'in open court' that you cannot require the public to come and watch a ceremony in which it takes no interest. So at the ballot there are seldom more than about twenty people present, including a few jurors who have skilfully noticed that the jury summons gives them the opportunity to be there, though it neither invites nor commands their attendance, and seems indeed to hope they won't come. The ballot is conducted in an office on the second floor. If, says Mr Baldock, a hundred people presented themselves one day and wanted to witness the proceedings, the ceremony would have to be adjourned to some convenient and vacant court room. It would mean, perhaps, that for an hour or two that court room would not be available for its normal and urgent business of conducting criminal trials; and someone would wait that much longer down in the cells for his case to be heard. It seems unlikely to happen. The present system, in operation since April 1965, is a great improvement on the former practice of summoning all the jurors to court on the first day of the session, merely for the purpose of dividing them into juries and telling all except those needed on that day to return at a later date. Today the jurors do not attend on 'ballot day' unless they want to; which in effect means that the only ones to attend are those – a very small number – who want to contest a rejection by the Sheriff of their applications for excusal.

There are still occasions when the Court has to arrange for the overnight accommodation of a jury that must not be allowed to separate. Such occasions are now rare. Until 1940 no murder jury was allowed to go home during a part-heard trial whatever stage it had reached. Later this was reduced to the detention of juries only in cases (of any kind) where the judge had actually begun his summing-up. And today the only occasion for detaining a jury is when it has actually retired to consider its verdict, and has gone on doing so until so late an hour that, in the opinion of the judge, it is time that everyone (except the jury) went home. Then the Court must find hotel or other accommodation for twelve jurors, preferably in rooms so situated as to make their supervision reasonably possible. They are strictly reminded (they will have heard it before) that they must not talk about *anything* to anyone other than their ushers and fellow jurors. Detained jurors were until recently advised not to discuss even with each other the details of the case they were trying; but a jury which is in the middle of considering its verdict could, it may be thought, hardly employ its time better. (The jury in the Great Train Robbery trial were out for sixty-seven hours.)

But if an embattled jury gives any signs, even late in the evening, that agreement is just possible, then hope deferred occasionally prolongs the sitting into the small hours. And more than once an Old Bailey judge who has gone to bed for the night has had to be roused in order to take a verdict at two or three in the morning. In such circumstances the jury bailiff, too, has a long day. And it must be borne: in 1960 the judge in *R. v.*

McKenna (1 Q.B. 411) told his jury, late one night, that he was giving them ten more minutes to reach agreement, failing which they would have to be locked up until he returned to Court in the morning. They then took six minutes and said Guilty. The conviction was quashed on appeal on the ground that it is improper for the judge to put the jury under *any* sort of coercion to arrive at a verdict.

You could say, in fact, that coercion has disappeared from the jury system. Its place has been taken by commonsense and an atmosphere of shared responsibility, a development which ought to be fostered by jury bailiffs. Hidden decently away, the coercive apparatus is nevertheless still there, as became apparent to the defiant juror who was sentenced, as a very last resort, to three days in Brixton Prison. The suspicion that it's there is probably important to some jurors; but the knowledge that it's there is certainly important to every jury bailiff.

OLIVER MILTON

Court Usher

I suppose that the job of court usher is generally considered to be the lowest in any court of law, but in its own way it is quite an important post. An incompetent usher can cause a lot of extra work and worry to the clerk of the court and even, in some cases, to the judge himself. This can happen in many ways, such as by administering the wrong oath to a witness or, when asked for a particular exhibit, by handing up the wrong one.

I started court work in the days of Quarter Sessions, which have now been superseded by the Crown Courts. My title then was Court Crier and this was only one part of my job as an assistant Town Hall keeper. My duties at that time were similar to my present ones, with the difference that there was only one court crier no matter how many courts were in session. The court crier did not assume the duties of jury bailiff; the police were then responsible for these, although this practice varied in some courts.

A court crier was responsible for meeting the jurors as they reported for service. The clerk would read out their names and the crier would then count them into the jury box. Each juror had in front of him a copy of the New Testament and a card with the oath printed on it. They were then sworn in *en bloc* by repeating the oath together after the crier. This procedure was altered in January 1971 when the Crown Courts came into being. Now, when twelve jurors are in the box, the court clerk asks each one to stand up, to hold the book in his right hand and to repeat the oath from the printed card which is handed to him by the usher. If a juror cannot, because of nervousness or for any other reason, read the oath in the proper manner, he is requested by the judge to repeat it after the usher.

It is at this stage, though before the would-be juror has taken the oath, that prosecution or defence counsel can object to any juror. This is done by the counsel saying, 'Stand down for the Crown,' or simply, 'Stand down,' or 'Objection.' Counsel need give no reason for this and is allowed up to seven objections in any one case. It is for this reason, of course, that more than twelve summoned jurors are taken into court each time a new jury needs to be sworn in.

The text of the juror's oath has not altered since Quarter Session days. If a juror (or witness) for religious or other reasons wishes to affirm, he may do so. By affirming the juror solemnly promises to discharge his duty truthfully and responsibly but without invoking God. The usher will announce to the judge that the juror wishes to be allowed to affirm – some judges ask the reason for this, but others do not. The difference in the oath is that the juror says, 'I do solemnly, sincerely and truly declare and affirm that I will . . . etc.'

An usher is himself sworn in by the clerk when a jury is ready to retire to consider its verdict. He is asked, 'Do you swear by Almighty God that you will keep this jury in some safe and convenient place, that you will suffer no one to speak to them or speak to them yourself, unless it be to ask them if they are all agreed upon their verdict, without leave of the court?' The usher then remains outside the jury room until a verdict is reached, when a member of the jury will knock to signify this fact to the usher.

I remember an unusual occurrence during Quarter Sessions in a case of alleged theft from a car factory by an employee. After the jury had been sworn *en bloc* and prosecution counsel was about to open his case, a juryman suddenly stood up and stated that he held a responsible position in the same firm. Immediately seven others got to their feet and declared that they were also employed by the same company. They were, of course, discharged from the case and the court was smartly adjourned while other jurors-in-waiting were obtained.

An usher's duties can, naturally, vary from court to court. Although basic rules are laid down for procedure a court clerk can vary these within reason. For example, some clerks announce the adjournment of court for lunch or at the end of the day, but others will let the ushers do this.

An usher always meets the judge or his deputies on arrival at the court buildings, escorts him to his chambers, robes him and precedes him into court announcing, loudly and clearly, 'All stand, please,' or 'Be upstanding in court, please.' Some judges prefer to robe themselves, but personally I like to assist any judge or Recorder with robing and am happy to carry out any request he might make, such as posting letters or obtaining telephone calls for him.

Once the court is in session an usher is responsible for calling witnesses as counsel requests them, and for administering the oath to them. The oath, of course, can be administered on the New Testament, Old Testament, Catholic New Testament, or the Koran, etc., according to the faith of the witness. Copies of these books are usually kept in court. However, if it was, for some reason, not possible to supply the desired text, the witness or juror would be invited to affirm. If this invitation was refused, steps would have to be taken to obtain the necessary book.

The usher normally then sits between the clerk and the witness box, in a position from which he can easily hand exhibits and such like to the witness as and when is necessary. Such exhibits are sometimes shown to the jury on direction of the court and, in any case, they are entitled to have all exhibits in their room when considering their verdict. An usher is not responsible for looking after exhibits. During the lunch adjournment, the court accepts responsibility for them and locks the court room, or even places them in another locked room. If exhibits are of great value, they are placed in the custody of the police.

An usher is also responsible for keeping a certain amount of order in court. There are no guidelines as such laid down for 'keeping order', but an usher must ensure silence in court during the administering of the oath, and that there is no smoking in the public gallery etc. Any undue noise caused by conversation among solicitors' clerks or even by counsel should be dealt with by a reprimand of 'Silence in court.' I have never known this to fail yet. An usher keeps his eye on the jury box and tries to stop any giggling or other disruption by drawing the court clerk's attention to it. Similarly, he would draw the clerk's attention to any juror who looked faint or ill in the box and, in the event of a juror wishing to pass a written question to the judge, the usher will take this and hand it up to the Bench.

When court is not sitting, an usher also helps with certain office work, such as operating the copy machine or writing up jury summonses. These duties are done during normal office hours and are an expected rather than a formal aspect of the job. An usher is paid a basic wage of between £25 and £30 per week and takes home, on average, between £22 and £24. This sum is greater in London and probably in some other cities. The post can be obtained by application to any Crown Court office in the applicant's town of residence, and such applications are then passed to the administrative office in the circuit concerned.

I find my job both satisfying and interesting. One meets some very nice people indeed and one is treated with great respect by all members of the Bar, judges and Recorders. This makes one feel that one is playing an important part in the legal system. One also accumulates a great deal of knowledge of the law and of the criminal element in society. I believe that thereby one develops a greater understanding of life in general.

ALFRED EATON

Counsel

One year into Oxford and I could construe a passage of Justinian and manumit a Roman slave. Three years into the Honours School of Jurisprudence and I had heard (although my lazy literal mind tended to float off at the second ghostly whisper of Norman French) about hereditaments corporeal and incorporeal; privileges without profit and profits a prendre; dominant and servient tenements; wardships and liveries, primer seisins and ousterlemains; values and forfeitures of marriage, fines for alienations, tenures by homage, knight's service and escuage. Free socage or plough service; grand and petit serjeantry; tenure in burgage and gavelkind. Villenage, pure and privileged. Frankferm and feoffment; frank marriage and hotch pot; frank bank (or francus bancus); frankalmoign and tenure by divine service; frankincense, gold and myrrh.

For us reluctant medievalists, class of 'fifty-two, English legal history ended with the collapse of the feudal system. The white rose, the red rose, the white knight, the red Queen, the Abbotts and the villeins crept off into the shadows while the two Henrys Tudor, each with his gang of hustlers, set about restructuring English society. But for us these nasty Welshmen did not exist: our players had, to a man, been struck down on Bosworth Field. Dead but not to be buried for another four centuries and a quarter. It was not until 1925 that, with his monumental Law of Property Act (a statute at the thought of which every devout Chancery lawyer should cross himself as against the Evil Eye: gone are those marvellous complications, gone are those lovely loopholes) Lord Birkenhead put the feudal pieces back into their box, pronounced a valediction and finally screwed down the lid.

Only occasionally did our syllabus impinge upon the crude

world we would one day inhabit. We took in contract and tort but these lofty questions of liability and Remoteness, of Quantum and consideration; these measured judgments of the House of Lords; these exploding ocean liners and defective submarines provided an exalted introduction to the modest County Court practices in which most of us were likely to engage for the next ten years. We trained with the Royal Ballet in order to busk in Leicester Square. Then, as befits a subject which is generally thought to be too easy to deserve serious academic attention, along with elements of Roman law, right at the beginning of the syllabus, we did crime.

Off we went to Magdalen for two hours every week, to hear Rupert Cross lecture on Criminal Law. These lectures were justly famous and undergraduates from other schools would crowd in to hear Professor Cross's jokes (which I, after more than twenty years, can still recall in every juicy particular) and to admire – later to imitate – his delivery, half Churchill and half Jimmy Edwards. The material was promising too: crime looked as though it was going to be a lot of fun: there was this fellow who thought he was Humpty Dumpty and another who thought he was a boiled egg; then there were the two ship-wrecked sailors who ate up the cabin-boy. Privileged and insulated from actual madness, from actual starvation as we were we thought it all terrifically funny. And Professor Cross has been totally blind from birth.

Three years into Gray's Inn (I joined my Inn of Court while still a school girl, kept term while an undergraduate and was called to the Bar the year after I came down from Oxford) I had eaten thirty-six dinners, learned the ritual toasting in the mess and the well worn jokes of Grand Night; the proper way to pass the port. I had danced in an Elizabethan masque – a 'RIOT' it was called (oh the dear dead 'fifties when a riot meant a party, where parties were not political, and demos not invented) – before the Queen; drunk champagne – a very great deal of champagne on a very large number of occasions – in the dew-drenched gardens of Gray's Inn while the day's first buses trundled down Theobald's Road. I had absorbed the forensic atmosphere (which is the aim and object of eating the dinners) and the delicious catty gossip (which is the agreeable result of consuming the same). I had had my bottom pinched by my first Queen's Counsel – and good grief! After twenty years and generations of sweet girl graduates I am told the fellow's still at it, leering and wagging his prehensile members as they come up the escalator at Chancery Lane.

The life of the Inns of Court is a logical extension of the life of the University. Here is the same arcane hierarchy; the same hammer-beamed halls; the same protection from the elements, from proletarian anger and from bourgeois pressures; the same sunny courts and terraces to stroll in after lunch; the same veridian lawns shaded by monster mulberries; in-jokes to tell; midnight libations to pour; superb libraries with logical catalogues; visits from Royalty; expensive parties and in winter, round the fat Norman rump of the Temple Church, the smell of raw salt fog from the river mingling in evocative comity with a whiff of printers' ink from Fleet Street and the aroma of hot roasting chestnuts. He who cannot make All Souls may still pass a pleasant enough lifetime in the Temple.

I loved my legal education but I regret it very much. At the age of sixteen I was consumed by an austere passion for abstract concepts, the English constitution and the works of Walter Bagehot. Seven years later on my call to the Bar, my ascetic Jekyll had been totally debauched by a luxurious Hyde whose abiding passions were for expensive living, Palladian architecture, scandal, gossip and news. How splendid it is to belong to an elite. How amusing to understand the power structure within it. And how absolutely insufferable for anyone on the outside looking in.

It is easy to be seduced by an English institution – particularly if one is poor or young or insecure. The spotty youth with a cast in his eye will become the smartest Guardsman in the regiment; the raw new Labour M.P. from Moss side or Clyde Bank the most meticulous Parliamentarian. (This last was told me by General Sir Brian Horrocks who, as Black Rod, saw radicals come, radicals go, radicals seduced, debauched and converted.) It is not difficult for the Inns of Court with their musky complicated aphrodisiac appeal first to enfold and finally to defuse the fierce young law student from a northern grammar school. It was not difficult for the majesty of the English law – the magic of the elite – to seduce this particular silly girl graduate.

The appeal of Gray's Inn was so great that in my day many of its most faithful stalwarts were not lawyers at all. There were barristers who had been called but who had never practised, now working as civil servants, law reporters, accountants, experts on tax; there were even non-studying students of mature age who had no intention of qualifying or even of taking a preliminary examination, clubable men who loved to foregather and to dine in Hall. These were the greatest sticklers for etiquette, the most meticulous historians of their society, the ones who could be absolutely relied upon to take up the last tickets to a ball or a champagne supper. In the honoured society but never quite of if they had their own private jokes to make, their own tales to tell; they would appear agreeably surprised if a Lord Justice of Appeal or a Law Lord came in to dinner more than twice in the term: 'Devlin is becoming quite a Gray's Inn man,' they would say.

The really busy practitioner is, of course, unlikely to be doing with any of this elitism (having, as a rich man, attained an elitism of his own) as he scuttles from his Chambers to the High Court and off to the House of Lords. He will not know a Wren cloister from a Poulson façade and for him a flying buttress is the quickest jet time between the Trucial States and the International Court of Justice at the Hague. No matter. The pillars of our ancient and most cherished institutions are inevitably the second-rate.

For others – for those who recall, or who in time come to perceive, that the raw material of litigation is human misery – these cloud-capped towers, these gorgeous palaces, are already insubstantial. These lamps, with their soft yellow effulgence on a winter's evening which shone for Coke and Blackstone, for Dr Johnson and gentle Lamb, also illumined the darker paths of Judge Jeffreys, Carson and Hewart L.J.

Mervyn Griffith-Jones was my Master in the law. Kind, cold, correct, remote, straight-backed as though he wore a brace, meticulous in his paper work, perfect in his articulation, totally organized, totally disciplined, he was exactly what I needed to sober me up: exactly what I needed to bring me down to earth as I floated round the Temple pleasantly wondering who was going to fall in love with me next. As a matter of fact he frightened me very much, this man whose self-sufficiency I could not dent, this cool man who never even noticed what I looked like.

As his pupil I had access to all his papers (save those involving

Official Secrets) and went in to court with him every day. It was 1956: he was first junior Treasury Counsel which meant that ninety-nine per cent of his work consisted of prosecuting for the Director of Public Prosecutions. His home ground was the Old Bailey. He did murders, manslaughters, rapes, big robberies, heavy frauds. 'You can forget about the murders,' he told me as I fell upon my first volume of ghastly forensic photographs. 'Most of them are very sad and very sordid: family affairs. What you'll find really amusing is fraud.' Few counsel want to persecute some poor wretch who has strangled his unfaithful wife: crimes of violence have a depressing similarity. But to pit one's wits against a Poulson or a Savundra or the underwriter who has cooked the books at Lloyd's is something quite different.

The Old Bailey has its own hierarchial structure as incestuous as any other in the law. As the Crown Court for the whole of the Greater London Area it is enormously busy (crime being the most successful growth industry in the country today). In 1956 there were six courts sitting regularly; now there are thirty-two. In spite of this it still retains something of the atmosphere of a club. Heavy prosecutions for the Director of Public Prosecutions are handled by Treasury Counsel: prosecutions for the police by counsel drawn from a list selected by the Scotland Yard solicitor.

A handful of Chambers have a stranglehold on the extremely lucrative legal aid defence work. There is a Bar mess where the barristers eat lunch together, get the gossip, find out whose case is going to fight and whose is to fold. The judges are almost entirely drawn from the ranks of senior Treasury Counsel, which means from professional prosecutors. They lunch with the Sheriffs and Aldermen of the City of London but each day they will invite one or two members of the Bar to eat with them. Again, although we do not *eat* with policemen, the relationship between prosecuting counsel and the police is very close, particularly with senior members of the fraud squad. Officers in charge of complex cases will attend conferences in Chambers by a convenient and time-honoured waiving of the rule which forbids counsel to have any direct contact with witnesses in a case. Deals are commonplace whereby prosecuting and defence counsel meet together and work out a compromise: I will plead guilty to grievous bodily harm if you do not proceed with your allegation of manslaughter. Counsel then see the judge in his private room. He blesses the arrangement, while agreeing on his part to pass a reduced sentence. At its best the system can save public time and money; at its worst it looks like a carve-up. When I wrote about it in my play *The Portsmouth Defence* I got into awful trouble: one silk told me I was a rotten little beast who had spoiled it for everyone.

Outsiders find the whole thing claustrophobic, at least. One practitioner distinguished in another court adapted the New England jingle to fit the bill ('Sam' is Sam Morton, Mervyn Griffith-Jones's brother-in-law, who was next to him in the hierarchy of Treasury Counsel).

How nice to be back at the Bailey
Where a wink is as good as a nod,
Where Sam speaks only to Mervyn
And Mervyn speaks only to God.

The whole system is weighted in favour of the prosecution. Prosecuting counsel may mix with the police, while if defence counsel associated with their witnesses they would be liable to disciplinary action; judges are drawn from the ranks of prosecuting counsel. There is only one thing which prevents the Old Bailey becoming a conveyor belt to prison and that is the independence of the jury.

All these bald heads, all these badged blazers, all these folded copies of the *Daily Telegraph* and *Mirror*: this token minority of bewildered housewives in their Conservative ladies' hats! These were our jurors: this was the imponderable factor in the machine of justice; this bullied multitude called to the Bailey on the first day of the session, lectured, hectored, marched hither and thither by small men in uniform enjoying to the full their recurring power trip. Mervyn – who although a man of the Establishment was also a man of the Constitution – held the jury in the greatest possible respect and treated each one with elaborate courtesy. In my six months' pupillage he gave me three pieces of advice – instructions, rather. One: to join the Inns of Court Conservative and Unionist Association and learn to play golf. Two: not to wear pink gloves to the Old Bailey. Three: never to put my hands in my pockets while addressing a British jury. Oddly enough it seems always to be the trendy young radicals who treat their jurors with contempt: hands in pockets, stomachs exposed. I remember one such opening his case with these words: 'Members of the Jury, it is often said that jurors are not intelligent enough to understand the merits of the alternative defence.' Silly man! Whatever the merits of his client's case, after an opening insult like that what jury would do anything but convict? Lord Devlin once described the typical juror as 'male, middle-aged, middle-minded and middle-class'. The most effective advocates are those who remember this and pitch their arguments accordingly.

The relationship between advocate and jury is like a shortlived but intense love affair which has to be conducted entirely in public.

Bold lover, never, never canst thou kiss,
Though winning near the goal – yet, do not grieve;
She cannot fade, though thou hast not thy bliss,
Forever wilt thou love, and she be fair!

There is the moment of introduction when the jurors come to the book to take the oath. One has the right of peremptory challenge in seven cases: one strains to read each face, to detect any sign of prejudice – and one has only about ten seconds in which to act. It is traditional to challenge women in cases of rape or homosexual assault, on the grounds that they might be too upset or shocked to return a rational verdict. I never saw the validity of this argument and was always delighted to have women on my juries: male bonding frightened me far more. By the time I came to make this decision I was doing almost entirely defence work and the one I'd challenge would be the man carrying the *Daily Telegraph*, symptom of a closed mind, or wearing a regimental tie.

The jury sworn, there comes the time of wooing. Knowing that I would never make a Patrick Hastings or even a Victor Durand, I decided to base my advocacy on the act of Lena Horne. I would pick out one susceptible-looking fellow and say it all to him, trying to eat him up with my eyes and arguments. If he started nodding his head I'd know that we were home and dry: if he wouldn't let me catch his eye I would know that we were down the drain. It was always easier to get one's way with a fresh jury at the beginning of the session. After two or three weeks' service one's jury starts to get a bit cynical: it will know, for example, that if no mention is made of a defendant's character this must mean that he has a criminal record, it will be getting doubtful about the busy long arm of coincidence around the courts and bored by constant appeals to its commonsense.

The affair ends. One is accepted or rejected: the jury are discharged and one can never know the reason for the verdict. It is acutely frustrating. Was it the rubbish one talked or one's client's face that led to this disaster? Only once, at Winchester Assizes, did I nearly find out. A juror invited me for a drink. I longed to go and to hear blow for blow exactly what had been said in that jury room, but some residual propriety in my normally improper breast forced me to refuse. I regret it to this day.

Six years after leaving the Bar, years spent living a totally different kind of life in a different country, I came back to the Old Bailey. The occasion was the trial of the Kray brothers and I came not as an advocate (although I knew the brethren well as old clients) but as a writer. I saw the scene through different eyes. The pomp and circumstance, the judge's procession, the nosegays, the ritual announcements touched no chord in heart nor mind, rather they frightened and depressed me. What once I would have thought witticisms from the Bench now struck me as examples of abominable rudeness. And the barristers, some of them giants of my youth, now seemed ponderous, incompetent, out of tune. I tried to convey what I felt in my play *The Traffic Warden's Daughter* when Agape Lianos, wife of a Greek ship owner, having earned the praise of counsel and judge, turns on the system: 'Old men in drag, young men in funny uniforms, all *this* I find too absolutely ridiculous.'

Only in one thing am I constant and that is in my feeling of total admiration for the jury. Out of the shambles of the Kray trial – putting aside prejudice, intimidation, boredom, class animosity, living legend – the jury returned a rational verdict. Would Mr Justice Melford Stevenson, had he been empowered to try it alone, have done as well?

The issues to be determined by a jury are very rarely complex. In most cases the question is a simple one: who is telling the truth? Even fraud, when one comes to examine it, usually presents a simple pattern – far simpler than the pattern of legitimate commerce. A lawyer is no more fitted to determine who is telling the truth than a doctor or dustman. No amount of legal training can teach us commonsense, give us a nose for integrity.

Most courts of summary jurisdiction are now run by stipendiary magistrates. In the main they work very well, but where there is a conflict of evidence, where there is a chance of acquittal, every advocate worth his salt will advise his client to go for trial by jury. However well a stipendiary starts, almost inevitably there comes a time when the prejudices harden and the mind closes. It is in the nature of the job. Abolish jury trial and the courts of the country would be run by glorified stipendiaries who would be – as Lord Goddard, the greatest protagonist of jury trial of his generation, pointed out – the disgruntled failures in their profession. Precious little justice would flow from that quarter.

Since Throckmorton's case in 1554 the courage of English juries has been the one golden thread in the black canvas of the law. I understand now why legal history ended with Bosworth Field; the rest is too frightful, too shaming to think about. Every reform, every concession to humanity almost, was resisted to the last by Bench and Bar, by the juggernaut weight of a backward-looking profession. For five hundred years the jury and the jury alone stood against the power of the sovereign, of the executive, of the Star Chamber, even against the monstrous tyranny of Coke's Common Law. Juries have been insulted by the Bench, patronized by advocates, starved, fined and even imprisoned by the executive. Those who would abolish trial by jury now, and for administrative convenience remove the last buffer between the citizen and an elitist profession, would do well to ponder the words of Blackstone written more than two centuries ago:

> So that the liberties of England cannot but subsist so long as this palladium remains sacred and inviolate; not only from all open attacks (which none will be so hardy as to make), but also from all secret machinations, which may sap and undermine it; by introducing new and arbitrary methods of trial; by justices of the peace, commissioners of the revenue, and courts of conscience. And however convenient these may appear at first (as doubtless all

> arbitrary powers, well executed, are the most convenient), yet let it be again remembered in the forms of justice, are the price that all free nations must pay for their liberty in more substantial matters; that these inroads upon this sacred bulwark of the nation are fundamentally opposite to the spirit of our constitution; and that, though begun in trifles, the precedent may gradually increase and spread, to the utter disuse of juries in questions of the most momentous concern.
>
> *Commentaries on the Laws of England*

Two hundred years later, Lord Devlin, for my money the greatest legal thinker of our age, expressed the same sentiments and gave the same warnings as the mighty Blackstone had before him. Anyone who claims that the love of liberty lies at the heart of his political philosophy would do well to ponder his conclusions:

> Each jury is a little Parliament. The jury sense is the Parliamentary sense. I cannot see one dying and the other surviving. The first object of any tyrant in Whitehall would be to make Parliament utterly subservient to his will; and the next to overthrow or diminish trial by jury, for no tyrant could afford to leave a subject's freedom in the hands of his countrymen. So that trial by jury is more than one wheel of the constitution; it is the lamp that shows that freedom lives.

NEMONE LETHBRIDGE

Appendix One

Police evidence and the presentation of prosecution cases

The first case I heard as a juror produced a feeling of sympathy for the police. A marked disparity appeared between the respective presentation of prosecution and defence cases, and this brought home the fact that the prosecution has the more difficult court-room task – the burden of proving a defendant guilty. The thought occurred that perhaps the police have to make do with any old counsel, the cream of barristers being reserved for the defendant at risk. Police evidence was consistent and dispassionate. Unbridgeable gaps began to appear in the defence, but a feeling, shared by other jurors, emerged that the Guilty verdict was reached in spite of prosecuting counsel's inadequate presentation.

However, as the eleven-day stint wore on, sloppy presentation of police cases became a constant factor in trial after trial. The explanation of this changed, however. Prosecuting counsels appeared to have to make bricks with the merest wisps of straw. The over-riding impression now created was that the simple fact of being a police officer placed their evidence beyond question and above suspicion. When challenged they were frequently rude and, as one acquittal followed hard on the heels of another, were visibly angry.

Inevitably, this led to an increasing disaffection among many jurors. The minority who had maintained from the start that 'There's no such thing as an honest copper' became smug. It was very difficult to argue against such blanket prejudice, even to retain a moderately open mind.

This distressing aspect of my jury service reached its worst point in a potentially important case of alleged theft. Two police officers flatly contradicted each other, to the increasing bewilderment of the jury. Cynicism set in. One began to lose sight of the important fact that evidence should not be fabricated in the longing for consistency: the first rule of lying with a partner is surely to agree on one version of the tale. Even so, four jurors held out for some hours because they simply could not believe that a policeman would lie in the witness box. But there was no other apparent explanation. It was no longer a question of deciding between the truth of prosecution and defence, the former split down the middle by the testimonies of the two officers concerned.

The jury felt certain that some reprimand would be delivered from the Bench. Perhaps even an inquiry would be indicated. Instead, congratulations were delivered to the senior officer who had subsequently been promoted.

My respect for the police was therefore seriously damaged by, of all things, serving on a jury. If my experience was not unduly exceptional, then it is no surprise that the police complain of the difficulty of obtaining Guilty verdicts before juries. The fault, however, lies with them and is not attributable to some inbuilt hostility in all juries. Only in one case out of six did the police evidence prevail and then, as I have said, in spite of poor presentation. It seems, therefore, that a genuine police case needs little help from counsel. A bad one, on the other hand, is presented with smiling arrogance, contradictions, begged questions and all. Juries, in my view, are doing their job much more conscientiously than some policemen – and that is why it is difficult for the police to secure convictions.

The triviality of cases

The inconsistencies in and bad presentation of police evidence have a bearing, I believe, on the jurors' second biggest grumble; that when they eventually get into court, they are frequently asked to sit in judgment on cases which are trivial. Juries can be divided, on this point, into two groups: those who deplore the waste of public money involved, and those who resent the waste of their time and effort. It is very difficult to argue, as one must, that a crime is a crime, irrespective of its 'importance' – which is usually assessed by juries in terms of the monetary gain to the defendant or the damage to the victim.

Juries asked to pronounce on the alleged theft of a few light bulbs or half-a-dozen toilet rolls constantly ask, 'Who cares?' or

'What does it matter?' This sounds like evidence in support of those pundits who constantly pronounce on the appallingly low standard of public morality, but it is not, I believe, that simple. This shoulder-shrugging attitude is the immediate result of boredom and frustration. The long hours, even days of waiting idly around produce a false eagerness when at last a jury is called. At last, its members feel, they have a chance to do their public duty, to justify their boredom, financial loss or whatever. When they are presented with a minor offence they inevitably feel let down and take on a dismissive attitude.

I have no doubt that this feeling can be and often is overcome where there is an indisputable case to answer. In my own experience, however, this feeling of indifference hardens when these trivial charges have every appearance of being trumped up. Juries display a lot of commonsense, which leads them to ask questions. Why did the police descend on the defendant and take a look round his spare bedroom? Obviously, because he is 'known'. No doubt they were looking for stolen property, but did not find it. Instead they seize upon a few unreceipted light bulbs or toilet rolls and arraign the man before a jury.

Such arguments may not be true, but in the absence of any evidence to prove that these objects have indeed been stolen, they are invariably used by jurors. And from them they draw the conclusion that certain people in our society are kept under surveillance and are regularly 'turned over'. Fair enough, but when the police's 'hunch', or whatever it is, proves to be unfounded, is it really necessary to clutter the courts with unprovable, trivial charges? It begins to look like police pique, or a blatant attempt to swell the records of conviction.

Again, juries become cynical, about the police and about the commission of crimes. There are moments during the unfolding of such cases when everybody begins to wonder if all this ritual, panoply and rhetoric can ever be justified. Why, jurors ask, are such cases allowed to reach full jury trial? The answer is obvious. Because the defendant has pleaded not guilty and has the right to such trial. The important question is who found there was a case to answer in the first place? Somebody, somewhere obviously shares the view that police cases are almost inviolable, no matter how scant and inconclusive the evidence.

The right of a jury to dismiss a case

On the tenth day of my jury service, in the middle of one of these same trivial cases, one of our number announced that a jury could, at any time after the completion of the case for the prosecution, bring in a unanimous verdict of Not Guilty on the defendant. Eleven of us did not, at first, believe him. The day before, he insisted, the jury on which he had then been serving had been so advised by the presiding judge. They had taken this advice as a virtual direction and, with some relief, had effectively stopped the trial.

This juror urged that we should adopt a similar line on our present case. There was some dissent but when, at the end of the prosecution case, he canvassed the jury, all were agreed that a note should be passed to the judge, telling him that we had reached a unanimous verdict and wished to hear no more. This was done and the case was stopped, to the evident delight of defence counsel, but not that of the judge.

Afterwards, I asked as many other jurors as I could if they knew about this right. It seems that only twenty-three of us knew about it – that is, the two juries having one man in common who actually exercised the right. To this day I do not know if this is indeed a right, given to all juries. It occurs to me that possibly it can only be used at the discretion of the judge. Was it for some reason expedient in that other case, in which the judge advised the jury of their right to do this, for the jury to dismiss the case, rather than for counsel to make the more usual submission?

I don't know, but whatever the letter of the law, there is no discernible reason why this right should be concealed from juries. Even if it is only operable in certain circumstances, these should be explained. Certainly, I can see that such a right could be open to abuse. As one juror said to me, if we'd known about it earlier, the process of justice would certainly have been speeded up.

Jurors are told virtually nothing about their duties and absolutely nothing about their rights. One feels like a second-class citizen, barely tolerated by the august personnel of the court. But the concealment by silence of this right of a jury to effectively dismiss a case seems to me iniquitous. By what right and on whose authority is it concealed? And if it is not, in fact, a right but only an occasional, emergency measure, then why conceal it? Juries are quite capable of understanding when they might invoke this device. To keep them in ignorance is only to increase their feeling that they are non-participants, an unreliable press-gang whose usefulness is merely the subject of exhortatory lip-service.

DULAN BARBER

Appendix Two

Law v. Truth

Before I'd done my stint of jury service, I suppose I'd taken an average, perhaps less than average, interest in trials. I had, with normal(?) curiosity, read the accounts in the press of the cases which made the headlines, or at least the news pages rather than the law reports. As a sometime editor with a publishing house well known for its thrillers, I'd read scores of crime novels though I was, and am, far from being addicted to the genre. Still, I thought I knew more or less what to expect. It soon became clear that there's little connection between the logical and patient ways in which crimes are solved in fiction, and the fuzziness and haphazard happenings of a Crown Court.

Was it naive of me to be surprised that the courts seemed more concerned with what is permissible in legal terms, with the niceties of the law, than in establishing the truth: whether or not the defendant did it? 'What is truth?' asked Francis Bacon's Pilate, and would not stay for an answer. This Pilate might have been a member of the legal profession.

Assuming it be presumed that God is infallible, that only He can legislate or pontificate without regard to evidence, must it be assumed that a learned judge and a jury cannot use their individual or collective intelligences? It is decreed, and in my experience judges are exemplary in pointing this out, that a verdict must be reached only in accordance with the evidence, and if there is reasonable doubt the jury must acquit.

So far so good, but if the jury feels that all the evidence which could be brought before them in fact has not been, they may try (if only to exercise the power they do at least in theory possess) to impose their will on the proceedings. And this is almost inevitably bound to irritate the judge. After all, the court is his; he is the dispenser of wisdom.

What power does the jury have? Consider if you will the following specific example. I served on a jury where the prisoner in the dock was accused of larceny. ('Larceny? Is that worse or better than ordinary burglary?' a fellow juror asked me.) The crucial witness was a woman called, let's say, Mrs Monteith, who almost definitely was the defendant's mistress. Had Mrs Monteith been asked whether the accused had brought the stolen goods to her she must have answered either yea or nay, and depending on her answer the jury's job would have been that much clearer. But Mrs Monteith was called neither for the prosecution nor for the defence. Assuming the lady was still of this world, this was something that not only bewildered members of the jury but frustrated us: *why* wasn't Mrs Monteith called, when her evidence couldn't fail but to make the case more intelligible?

It so happened that returning to the court after the lunchtime recess on the second day of the trial, I looked at the noticeboard just inside the main door of the building, on which were listed the cases currently being heard. They included, as well as the numbers of the courts and the judges presiding, the names of the defendants. In the notice pertaining to the case with which I was concerned, two defendants were listed: the prisoner in the dock, and Mrs Monteith.

I conferred with my eleven fellow jurors, and when we returned to the court room at once sent a note up to the judge: *On the notice board at the entrance to the court building there are listed two defendants in this case, the prisoner in the dock, and Mrs Monteith. May we ask what has happened to Mrs Monteith? Why isn't she in the dock?* His honour read the note, and re-read it. And perhaps re-read it again. His eyes raked the twelve of us. I was sure I was blushing, and that his eyes picked my face out. Was I the only juror foolish enough to meet his icy glare with a guilty look, or did we all feel at that moment equally in the dock? Presumably, I shall never know.

The judge spoke, to the effect that a member of the jury had asked him a question, and – this in a weary but tolerant way – he was bound to show the note to prosecuting counsel; which, via his learned clerk and then via the usher, he did. He then had the note passed by the usher to defending counsel. The suspense during these few minutes was tremendous, and I felt the resentment of everyone, including most members of the jury who presumably felt we should do as we were told, and not otherwise become involved.

The judge then asked permission of learned counsel to address the jury. 'One of you', he began ominously, holding my eyes with his like a predatory owl, 'has asked me a question.' I quite expected to be clapped in irons. And he continued, the tenor of his words being that the jury should do what it's told and not behave as amateur detectives because really they weren't very good at it. He didn't say this in so many words but the implication was clear.

It transpired that if a defendant changes his plea from Not Guilty to Guilty within twenty-four hours of the commencement of a trial he or she cannot appear as a witness either for the prosecution or for the defence. I would maintain that had this information been revealed voluntarily to the jury at the commencement of the trial we would have been substantially less perplexed as to what was going on. We would also, obviously, have accepted that the defendant and Mrs Monteith (who had been accused of receiving the goods alleged to have been stolen, and who had subsequently changed her plea from Not Guilty to Guilty) had come to a private arrangement between themselves.

As it was, we acquitted, largely I think because we felt irritated at having been kept in the dark on such a fundamental point.

If one were playing a game, however sophisticated a game, it might be considered not unreasonable that the rules are all important. As in any profession or occupation, what perhaps makes the law palatable to the bewigged practitioners is that there are rules and regulations to which they all adhere. But the name of the game is man's liberty, and any self-respecting jury (and in my experience juries are very self-respecting in so far as they approach their task with the utmost seriousness) will not be fobbed off with legal jargon or nonsense. If a jury can find out what its rights are it will employ those rights to the utmost. It ill behoves the law to keep the jury in the dark as much as it can, to imply – if only by omission – that really twelve laymen cannot understand the complexities of what is taking place in front of their eyes. If that were the case, the jury system should be abolished at once, as a travesty of justice. But of course it is not the case.

In short, the more open a court is with a jury, the more a jury learns by way of truth and honesty than by cleverness and guile, the more likely that jury is to arrive at a true verdict. And shouldn't counsel on both sides prefer that, in the long term? Even if they lose their case, they may win the next. Is it improper to suggest that to a jury a good counsel is one who reveals what's what as clearly as possible rather than (as happened in a case I heard) deliberately confuses the issue by pretending that there are three identical looking bearded Frenchmen living in the same house in Mill Hill?

The jury as ass

Dickens's Mr Bumble had it that the law is a ass; and from what I saw of the Crown Courts it was clear that the court reciprocated the sentiment as far as the jury was concerned; and the jury was an evil, if a necessary one. And evil because incompetent. Frankly, given the extent to which jurors are browbeaten, one can see why. But, it should be remembered, it is the jury which decides the verdict, although admittedly not the sentence. If the jury thinks that the evidence has been presented badly, that the judge's summing-up was unfair, the remedy lies in their hands. They *can* ignore everything they've heard, and decide that because the accused has an honest face they'll acquit. Or convict. Their decision is final, and the judge can only pour contempt on their heads. (A judge on a case which I heard as a member of a jury appeared so incensed that we had acquitted that he noisily and irrelevantly pointed out after the verdict was pronounced that the defendant 'had a string of previous convictions as long as your arm', as if that proved we should have found him guilty.)

If the courts were to treat the jury as being more intelligent, to credit them with understanding what they are about, as fair-minded human beings and citizens if not as legal luminaries, I believe juries would be less resentful in the jury room of the forces that seem to be against them in court. (And, of course, a respectable waiting room and a decent canteen would also assist the ego and morale of jurors, and therefore justice.)

I might have thought this view of the inferiority complex of the juror shared by few had it not been echoed by so many of my fellow jury panel members when I served, and indeed by so many of those we've been in correspondence with all over the country in connection with this book. Memo to counsel and judges: don't make the jury feel inferior. Flatter its intelligence and impartiality even. Remember that most jurors resent being there at all, and they're hardly making their living out of it as you are.

The period of time before which cases are brought to court
Each of the three cases which I heard as a member of a jury took over a year to be brought to court. No wonder the police witnesses could remember nothing without referring (with the judge's permission, only) to their little black plastic bound books, no wonder the defendant could swear with complete conviction that at the time the crime was committed he was drinking in the Sheep's Head with three companions, none of whom he'd set eyes on since.

If cases could be brought to court within a few weeks of the crimes being committed, it is likely that the evidence produced would be better, more detailed and more accurate, because the memories of witnesses would be reasonably free from subsequent fantasies and distortions. If the courts could catch up on their backlog of cases, and if, say, at this time next year cases could come to court within two or three months, I'd speculate that each case would be dealt with more expeditiously than at present and with a greater likelihood of the right verdict being obtained.

It will be argued that this is an administrative matter, and so it is. But because the freedom or otherwise of human beings is at stake, it is an administrative matter which surely must be put right urgently.

GILES GORDON

Select Bibliography

Authorities

W. Forsyth, *History of Trial by Jury* (1851)

W. S. Holdsworth, *History of the English Law* (1922)

F. Pollock and F. W. Maitland, *History of the English Law Before the Time of Edward I* (second edition, 1898)

J. B. Thayer, *Preliminary Treatise on Evidence at the Common Law* (1898), chapters 2-5

Blackstone, *Commentaries on the Laws of England* (mid-eighteenth century)

New Contributions

W. R. Cornish, *The Jury* (Allen Lane, London, third edition, 1963)

Lord Devlin, *Trial by Jury* (The Hamlyn Lectures) (Stevens, London, fourth impression, 1971)

Glanville Williams, *The Proof of Guilt* (Stevens, London, third edition, 1963).